MARRIAGE HOMILIES

Edited by LIAM SWORDS

Marriage Homilies

PAULIST PRESS
New York ● Mahwah

Published by arrangement with
The Columba Press, Dublin

First published in the United States by
PAULIST PRESS
997 Macarthur Boulevard
Mahwah, N.J. 07430

Library of Congress Catalog Card No: 85-62463

ISBN 0-8091-2785-7

Printed in the Republic of Ireland

CONTENTS

4. One-ness

5. Home making

6. Interchurch marriages

7. Mature Marriages

8. Anniversaries

PREFACE

Marriages, they say, are made in heaven. Marriage homilies, regrettably, have humbler origins. Few come without effort, an effort not always reflected in inspired words. Each marriage is unique. To reflect that uniqueness requires something more than easy familiarity with the couple's first names. For them it is a highly charged moment. For the homilist it is a rare opportunity to reach two individuals with God's saving word. The Word of Life must become words for life.

For the congregation of family and friends it is a time of celebration. But the occasion has more to offer than flowers and fashion, wedding-cake and banquet speeches. For many of them it is a time of recall. The homily could make it a time of renewal. Ironically, the priest whose homily is a dismal failure too often wows the guests with his after-dinner wit.

These reflective pieces make no claims other than that they are the results of others' toil. If they don't always inspire, they may at least challenge our acceptance of mediocrity. A little sweat and the grace of God can work wonders. The effective homily is the child of both. There is no substitute for either. God won't grudge the over-taxed preacher a helping hand. This collection offers just that.

Liam Swords

1
Love

Dance of love

Reading: 1 Cor 13:1-8

'It's love that makes the world go round' the song says. Dante put it more poetically in his *Divine Comedy* writing of 'the love that moves the sun and other stars'. Both have the same message – the ultimate mystery of being is love. That is what keeps the world going. Every creature is drawn to give itself in love, to surrender to the attraction of love. This is the rhythm of creation, as fundamental as the ebb and flow of the tides pulled by the moon. So too living cells divide and come together again. At all levels of life the male is drawn to the female and the female to give self back to the male. Throughout the whole universe runs the dance of love.

We also are swept along in this dance of love as every human being has a longing to be loved and to love, an inbuilt natural urge and need to receive and to give love. For there is a double movement – to and fro, back and forth – because receiving and giving are both parts of loving. And only those who have love in them are fully free in themselves to give it.

A child is a total receiver, wide open for loving. In God's plan, the proper nature of things, the small person experiences love from father and mother and so grows to like and love self. A child who is loved from the start is set up for life and as an adult is emotionally secure and strong enough to relate maturely to others. Self-esteem is not indulgence or selfishness. In the sentence from the gospel, 'love your neighbour as yourself', we stress the words 'love your neighbour' without paying sufficient attention to the words 'as yourself'. These make the point that the standard for our attitude to others begins with the right one to ourselves. A person who has been loved, loves self and is free to love.

We can do no better than offer the couple our prayers that love will make their world go round and that the warmth of the sun and the beauty of the stars will encircle their lives. We hope they will never cease learning how to be lovers in sharing what they have and what they are in their good times and in their bad times, working through the inevitable disagreements and frictions of married life towards greater closeness. 'I love you' does not mean 'I own you'. Love can never be forced on another or extracted from another. As a gift freely given it is freely received.

There was a custom centuries ago for a bride's ring to carry on the inside the inscription 'In Christ and thee my love shall be'. It is a lovely prayer for any couple.

We put their love for each other within the golden circle of the love of Christ.

Tony Baggot SJ

God's image and likeness

Readings: Gen 1:26-31. Ps 128. Jn 16:5-15

There are two accounts in Genesis of the creation of man. The second account talks about God putting man into a deep sleep and taking a rib to make a woman. That story seems to suggest that woman was an after-thought, but the first account takes the view that, far from being made in the image of man, woman is essential to making the image of God. This story says. . .

> God created man in the image of himself
> In the image of God he created him
> Male and female he created them.

There is no question there of woman being secondary. Mankind is made in two complementary sexes, male and female.

When God had created *them* – not him – the first thing he did was to bless them. Then he married them saying 'be fruitful and multiply and fill the earth'. Then he gave them a wedding present. . . the whole world. He said, 'Be masters of the fish of the sea, the birds of the air and all living animals on the earth.' Here we have the story of the wedding at the very beginning of the world, delayed only for the six days so that all the presents would be ready for the first married couple. And the wedding presents and the couple were checked out by God himself. 'And God saw all that he had made, and indeed it was very good.'

We are here today to do again what God did at the very beginning of the world, to bless God's image and likeness, to bless them male and female. The question is: what is meant by being the image of God? How are these two people the image of God? What did God see in the first two people that he made his image? It cannot have been the size and shape of their bodies, for that relates human beings to God's other creatures.

What he saw was the love between the man and the woman, their delight in each other, and their determination to remain together. He saw two distinct and equal beings held together by love. He saw a community of love. The Blessed Trinity, Father, Son and Holy Spirit, is such a community of love.

The love which binds together the Trinity is so vast that the creation of the entire universe is as natural to God as the birth of a child to a human couple.

When we look at this couple the most obvious thing about them is their love for each other. That love, which holds them together for life, is what makes them the image of God. All of us who see them happy together in love are being given a chance of looking at the nature of God.

Cathal & Norah O Boyle

The most effective sermon

Readings: Gen 2:18-24. Ps 127. 1 Cor 12:31–13:8. Matt 19:3-6

Alleluia, alleluia,
As long as we love one another
God will live in us,
And his love will be complete in us
Alleluia

That beautiful passage from St Paul sounds a warning note for me, especially 'If I have all the eloquence of men or angels, but speak without love, I am simply a gong booming or a cymbal clashing'. That is a rather terrifying thought for a preacher. None of us can take it for granted that we speak with the kind of love that Paul preached so eloquently. We can only pray the Holy Spirit to pour it into our hearts.

However our Lord himself speaks to us much more eloquently today through the voices of this couple than through any words of the preacher. Their mutual expression of love for each other, he says, signifies his love for us. That is very consoling, very reassuring. How grateful we are to them for giving us this sign of the love of Christ for his people.

It is only through our love for each other that the love of Christ can live in us. We are living in a world where a great many people tell us that they do not believe in God. Wherever there is genuine human love there God is present. For God is love. And whoever genuinely loves is loving God whether he/she can name him or not. For God is love.

It does, of course, add a new depth and richness to our lives when we realise that love comes from God. We see the whole wide world in a different light when we see it as God's gift to us. We have gratitude in our hearts for the gifts that we have received. And the greatest gift of all is the gift of love. For that we are most deeply grateful and we pray that it may be of such sterling quality as to abide forever.

In being grateful to God we are also grateful to our parents. So while expressing gratitude to this couple for giving us a sign of Christ's love for us we thank their parents also. Under God, it is they who have given them the capacity to be ministers one to another of this great sacrament.

Henry Peel OP

Kings and commons

Readings: 1 Jn 4:7-12. Lk 24:13-35

In the Greek Church the bride and groom wore crowns. They saw marriage as a coronation, a crowning of love. The bride and groom were king and queen for the day – king and queen in a kingdom of friendship, a kingdom of celebration, of joy. And there was a deeper meaning too – their kingship said that for the two human beings the prayer 'thy kingdom come' had been realised. There's the flavour of heaven about a wedding. At that moment two people love each other so much that they are prepared to give their lives to and for each other. That's God's kind of generosity – a love that is beyond reason and longer than life and stronger than death.

This love they pledge is not a feeling – nobody can promise a feeling. It is not a feeling but a policy. With great daring two human beings are about to defy time and circumstance and selfishness and proclaim that whenever, wherever, however, whoever, I am for you, all for you, now and always.

It is a moment of complete generosity, of generosity that has thrown caution to the winds, of generosity that is only possible when love inspires it. When two people can be as generous as that, when there is goodness like that, then whatever else is true this is true – that God is present at this moment. He is present to bless it, to be part of it and to treasure it – for it is his sort of moment, the sort of moment he spoke of when he said 'A man can have no greater love than to lay down his life for his friends'.

God knows it is not an easy gift to give for great generosity never comes cheap. It is a promise that can only be made in humility and with a cry for help – the help of God. And so God says, 'I am part of your gift and your love. I will be this day and always.'

Of course, and their majesties realise this, coronations are for one day and kings and queens cannot live on thrones forever. The crown gives way to curlers in the hair, and there isn't much majesty in a king who can't find his socks. But marriage is for every day and for all kinds of days. So we rejoice in this day but we look beyond it. Today is the beginning of a journey. A journey of two people like the one in the gospel, two people on a voyage of discovery, with certain uncertainties, wise enough to be unsure, walking along in the company of God, but often, as we all are, unaware of him, and coming to know him slowly, through each other, in the breaking of bread.

Through each other and in their own home and in everyday things they will meet goodness and love – these are simply other names for God. And they will realise that he is the third who walks beside them on their way.

We wish them a long journey and we hope it doesn't feel long. But may they learn from every blind alley and find new meaning from every misdirection. If there are Calvaries to be climbed may they help each other and come closer together in the climb, and from the vantage point of that height may they see more clearly and love more dearly.

And finally, may they have the gift of compassion – for each other first of all and then, as people acquainted with and respecting pain, for others. May their words be comfort and their hands healing and their home happiness, and their lives grace for each other and for their friends and for all they meet.

Thomas Waldron

Love never ends?

Reading: 1 Cor 13:1-13. Rom 5:1-5

A fuddy-duddy elephantine thing

In the stormy 60's when everything traditionally sacred seemed 'up for grabs', some theologians suprised us with a seductive theory. To decide what is moral, to act in ethical fashion, to live as a Christian, you don't need the thousand and one principles of the past; you can dispense with all that paraphernalia, all that baggage, of right and justice and so on. All you need is love. Why? Because love has an inbuilt compass that 'homes' it unerringly on to the essence of an issue, the pith of a problem. Love and you've got it made.

In response to the compass theory, an Anglican canon with wisdom and wit told a touching story, the story of an elephant, a loving elephant. It seems that this particular elephant noticed an ostrich leave her nest to get a drink of water. The elephant rumbled over to the nest and, out of pure love, sat on the ostrich eggs to keep them warm. 'Love,' observed the canon, 'can be a fuddy-duddy elephantine thing.'

My sermon will not play down St Paul's paean to love. I intend simply to uncover two profound truths that lie hidden in that matchless song of praise. First, love – specifically, wedded love – is tough. Second, such love is possible only if you are not two but three.

I
The sounds between the spaces

First then: Love – specifically, wedded love – is tough. I mean a dictionary definition of 'tough': love makes heavy demands on you; love is extremely difficult to cope with. Read Paul's ode to love again, but this time listen to what Castaneda called the space between the sounds.

Of course 'love is patient and kind'; but lovers are dreadfully impatient and can be terribly unkind. I chafe and fret if you keep me waiting – for breakfast or the bathroom, for a theatre curtain or a sports contest to begin. I know you so intimately that, if I'm not careful, I dissect you the way a critic cuts up a pitiful film for the newspaper. Naturally, it's for your own good, so you can be as perfect as I am.

Of course 'love is not jealous'; but lovers can and do grow green-eyed with jealousy. I grudge you your job, its fascination for you, the hours it tears you from me. I envy you your friends; they seem so

16

much more interesting than mine. I am suspicious of the way you smile at someone attractive – a smile that should be reserved for me.

Of course 'love is not rude'; but lovers can be barbarously boorish. Familiarity, the ages tell us, breeds contempt. I see so much of you that I neglect you in a group without a gram of guilt. Your anniversaries, once sheer delight to me, now burden my memory. My touch and my kiss have turned routine; I get awfully good at play-acting.

Of course 'love does not insist on its own way'; but lovers get rigidly set in their ways. Age plays tricks with my memory. Your pleasure, that once delighted me, is now an irritating whim of yours. Monday nights are for TV football; you knew that when you married me. Don't expect me to entertain your friends; they bore me; they're absolutely ignorant of corporation law. And stop rumpling my hair; I just combed it.

Of course love 'rejoices in the right', rejoices in the truth; but lovers come to tears and tantrums on what is right, on what is true. Understandably at times; for right and truth do not come out of a computer. Paul is talking about truth that is the very heart of Christianity, truth that expresses itself in holiness. This can divide you, especially when you disagree on Christianity itself, on the person and meaning of the God-man.

Of course 'love believes all things, hopes all things, endures all things'; but lovers doubt, lovers despair, lovers find one another difficult to endure. For the years take their toll of us. Sad experience can sour us. A dear one dies, in childbirth or in Auschwitz, and God dies too. The green years of youth and promise fade, and hope can wither as well. And how will you endure me when the firm lines turn to fat and I no longer remind you of Burt Reynolds?

Perhaps 'love never ends'; but, dear St Paul, ever since you wrote that lovely line, countless lovers have fallen out of love.

II
Love is a gift

Now this is not a jeremiad against marriage, a salute to the single life. Quite the contrary. The flaws that can afflict lovers, the comedy of errors, the tragedy of dismembered love – all this is important and pertinent because it leads into the second profound truth hidden in the passage plucked from Paul. The love Paul is lauding, the love that is patient and kind, never jealous or rude, the love that does not insist on its own way and rejoices in the right, the love that believes and

17

hopes and endures simply everything, the love that never ends – this is not a love that bride and groom create. In this section of his letter to the Christians of Corinth, Paul is speaking of spiritual gifts – I mean gifts freely given by the Holy Spirit, given by God. And so he speaks of wisdom and knowledge, of faith and healing, of prophecy and tongues; he mentions apostles and teachers and administrators in the Church of God. In this context he suddenly cries: 'And I will show you a still more excellent way' (1 Cor 12:31), a still more excellent gift, more excellent than any of the above. The great gift of the Spirit, the gift that surpasses all the rest, is the gift of love.

Here the crucial word is 'gift'. This kind of love the couple do not fashion themselves, out of their natural talents, their native characteristics. High IQs they have, lovable personalities; generous they are, willing to share, anxious to please, touchingly concerned each for the other. But if on this alone they were to base their life together, I would be less than optimistic.

Fortunately for them, the love that links them in wedded oneness, the love St Paul extols, leaps light-years beyond those splendid traits. God's gift to you today is the love Paul proclaimed to the Christians of Rome: '. . . hope does not disappoint us, because God's love has been poured into our hearts through the Holy Spirit which has been given to us' (Rom 5:5). What makes your love for each other particularly precious, what lends high promise for love that never ends, is God's love. Not somewhere in outer space, but within you. God loves you; God lives in you; God ties your love to his, ties it to the love that led him to give his own Son to a bloodstained cross for you.

Such love – God's love for you, God's love within you – such love is genuinely a gift. You may not demand it; you do not deserve it; you cannot buy it. God gives it out of sheer goodness. It is his pledge that through the bittersweet years that lie ahead you need never be alone, that your love will endure all things, can indeed be endless, if you are not two but three, if your own wondrous love for each other is carefully, caringly cradled in God's love.

Therein lies my one word of caution: God's gift of love, though priceless, is not costless. Like all love, God's love makes demands on you. Perhaps his heaviest demand, his most constant demand, is the plea every lover wings to a beloved: Don't forget me. When you leave this chapel, this gentle reminder of crucified love, you will return to a fascinating world. I mean an absurd little earth, where a billion humans fall asleep hungry; a glorious globe that was freed from slavery by the crucifixion of its God; a paradoxical planet that nurtures love and hate, despair and hope, scepticism and faith, tears and smiles, wine and blood; a creation of divine love where men and women die for one another and kill one another. It is here that you must live your love, here that you must share your love, especially with so many who experience far more of Christ's crucifixion than of his resurrection. It can be an intriguing adventure in human love *if.* . . if you forget not the divine love that alone makes for endless love.

Walter J Burghardt SJ

Reprinted from *Grace on Crutches,* by Walter J. Burghardt SJ, by permission of the Paulist Press.

An immortal diamond

Readings: Song of Songs 2:8-10, 14, 16, 8:6-7. Ps 84. Col 1:25-28.
Jn 15:12-16

St Patrick prayed: 'Christ on my right hand, Christ on my left hand.'

It is an apt thought for any Christian couple on the threshold of marriage. When you pledge love and your lives to each other as husband and wife, you will also be taking on the responsibility of being channels of grace for each other, of supporting each other in faith and hope, in short, leading the other to Christ.

Love for each other mirrors Christ's love for his people. He loved us to death. But after his death the angel at the empty tomb told the apostles, 'He is risen, he is not here'. He suggested that they look for him in Galilee, among the community of believers, where he is today, among his people.

In a very special way he is present in this church with this bride and bridegroom, as if resting a hand on both their shoulders saying, 'I am here with you, encouraging and supporting you in this sacrament, and I want to remain with you and draw you closer to each other in my love.'

If it is true that his presence in the community of believers means that Christ has no other face except mine and yours, no other hands except our hands, no other heart except our hearts, then a husband and wife must, before all others, be the face, hands and heart of Christ for each other. In this way they enable themselves to achieve a happiness which is deep and satisfying in this life, and eternal in the next. We are witnessing an event today which has eternal implications. This is the start of a story without an end.

The diamond engagment ring was a symbol, a public statement of the love for each other. Like any precious stone, that diamond had to be cut, shaped and polished the better to display its sparkling brilliance and beauty. You will also have to work at developing and shaping your lives together as man and wife, and that little gem will always be a reminder of the enthusiasm and happiness of these early days, and a pointer to the future to treasure each other more and more.

But rings and stones, no matter how precious, are still finite material things. Our prayer is that your love for each other may be, as Gerard Manley Hopkins wrote, 'an immortal diamond'.

Dermod McCarthy

Happy ever after

Readings: 1 Jn 4:15-19. Ps 127:1-5. Jn 13:13-35.

One of the most obvious things about young people getting married is that they are in love. Nobody is in the slightest surprised at this state of affairs. Love between married people is taken for granted. Now that is precisely what should not happen. Love should be noticed and attended to, especially by those who are getting married. Love demands all the attention we can manage, for God is love.

In fairy stories this day would be the end of a love story. 'They were married and lived happily ever after' is a standard way to finish a story. The problem with the fairy story ending is that there is no automatic guarantee that married people will live happily ever after. If the love lasts ever after then there will be happiness ever after. If the love stops tomorrow the happiness stops tomorrow. Love alone is the guarantee of happiness, and God is love.

Now that these two people are married their vocation in life is to live together in love for the rest of their lives. Everyone knows that love is hard to keep alive, it depends on constantly keeping the beloved in mind. Setting up a new home, meeting the new bills, making new friends, all of these things are going to take up some of the attention of both these people. If anything drives your spouse out of your mind for any length of time then your love is beginning to fade. Constant attention to the beloved is what makes a courtship, and what makes a courtship makes a marriage. When people are courting the worries of the world are of secondary importance. There is no room for selfishness or any other sin if love fills the heart, for God is love.

'Whoever lives in love lives in God and God lives in him.' Here we have two people in love. God is here in them because they love one another. They are keeping Christ's commandment that they should love one another. If they can sustain that love God will always be with them. God will help them to sustain their love if they ask him. God is the first and greatest of all lovers and will only live in us if we invite him. He will live happily ever after with this couple if they ask him, and they will live happily ever after with him. That, then, is our prayer for them, that they live happily ever after in love, for God is love.

Cathal & Norah O Boyle

Sexual love

Readings: Gen 1:3, 2:25, 4:1. 1 Cor 6:13-14. Jn 8:1-11

There is much suspicion in Christian circles on the current emphasis on sexuality. Firstly, it is seen as pleasure run amok. Secondly, the presence of widespread birth regulation has severed the intimate link between sexual intercourse and procreation. So at the present moment Christianity is perplexed. If the predominant link between sex and procreation is severed, as 99 out of 100 acts of intercourse are deliberately non-procreative, then what is the meaning of sex? Can it be that the image of God in man is expressed fully in sexual pleasure alone? These are fundamental questions which need careful thought. What follows is one such line of thought.

Sexual intercourse is a body language of love. When two people are making love they are talking to each other. In the biblical language they are getting to know each other. But what are they saying to each other with their bodies?

They are saying at least five things. In the course of coitus a couple are experiencing pleasure and they want to thank each other for that joy. They do this with or without words. Thus, sexual intercourse is an act of *thanksgiving*. Secondly, when couples have made love they want to repeat it immediately, the next day or the day after. Implicit in this desire is the hope that their spouse will want them again. Now it is a recurrent act of *hope*. Thirdly, in the course of the day couples hurt each other. Some of this hurt is forgiven and forgotten immediately, but some pain can remain, and it is coitus that takes it away. So sexual intercourse can be an act of *reconciliation*. Fourthly, coitus is the most economic and powerful way by which a man makes a woman feel a woman, and a woman makes a man feel a man. It is therefore a recurrent act of *affirmation of sexual identity*. Fifthly, every time a couple make love they are saying to each other that each is the most recognised, wanted and appreciated person in the other's life. Here it is one of the most powerful means of *personal affirmation*.

Thus, each act of intercourse has the potential of giving *life* to the couple and on a few occasions new life begins. Sexual pleasure no longer stands alone, but it is at the service of the life and love of the couple, strengthening their marital bond.

Another feature also emerges from this point of view. It can be seen that sexual intercourse is an extraordinarily rich experience. Its richness does not come from physical pleasure but from the strength the pleasure gives to the relationship of a couple. The couple need a continuous, reliable and predictable relationship to make the best use of intercourse. Hence all transient, promiscuous sex is wrong not because of the illicit use of pleasure but because that pleasure is not serving two people in a truly human way. Authentic sex needs a continuous relationship to do justice to its richness. It finds that in the relationship we call marriage. It cannot find that in the transiency of fornication and adultery.

Jack Dominian

Share, care and be fair

Readings: 1 Cor 13:1-13

I would like to leave with you three words as reminders for the years ahead. They summarise, I think, what God expects of you as husband and wife; they also contain the basic ingredients of a succesful marriage.

First of all, *share*. You obviously will share many things after you leave this church. The congratulations and gifts of guests are a start; the wedding cake is a symbol. But you will and must share much more – your time, your money, your bodies, your home. But above all you need to share your feelings – the joys and sorrows, the successes and failures. You need to communicate inner feelings, to get them out of one heart into the heart of the other. When you feel neglected or angry, you somehow must convey this, even when it is painful; and when you feel taken for granted or are hurt, you also must communicate those sentiments, whatever the cost. A practical suggestion to make sure you do communicate, you do share: Every day spend a few moments simply talking, listening to one another.

The second word is *care*. You may share or communicate perfectly, but unless you care, it makes little difference. You may know well what troubles your wife, but unless you care, you will do nothing about this. And, you too may recognise what irks your husband, but unless there is concern or care in your heart, you will have no desire to improve the situation.

Care is a synonym for love. And love entails giving. Ask your parents. They will, I am sure, tell you that marriage is a give-take, a giving-receiving relationship and that there is in it more giving than receiving. If you care, you will be more concerned about making each other happy than in having your own way; if you love, you will be more intent upon pleasing each other than in fulfilling your own desires. Care or love means unselfish giving. This is really the essence of married life. A second practical recommendation: Let the last words of each day, regardless of what has gone before, be 'I love you'.

Finally, be *fair*. All is bliss now, but all won't be heaven tomorrow. There will be disagreements, arguments, misunderstandings; there will be hurt feeling and perhaps harsh words. For you both are imperfect creatures who sometimes fail and aggravate others. These differences can either spoil and destroy your love or strengthen and deepen it. If you quickly reconcile, if you swiftly heal wounds, then your love will plunge to a new level and your joy increase. But if you allow these conflicts to continue, the wounds to fester, then misery in marriage will be your companion and marital ruin your destiny. My third bit of advice: Always make up before you fall asleep. 'Never let the sun go down on your anger.'

Even if you share, care, and are fair, you will still not find perfect happiness. No one has that in this life. But I think all of us here can assure you of as much joy as God gives men in our world. And you can be certain that the Lord will stand next to you always and give you his support whenever it is needed. He is present in the sacrament you are now going to receive and he promises to be with you all the days of your life.

Joseph M Champlin

Reprinted from *Christ Present and Yet to Come* by permission of Orbis Books, Maryknoll, New York.

Faith and love

Reading: 1 Jn 4:7-12

Faith is something born from love:
the faith between you both is born from the love between you,
and that faith between you both brings you to this day of hope
promised to one another –
because you have been awakened into surprise by one another,
and your faith together is born from that surprise of being loved.

The other faith is born from the surprises of another love:
it starts from God's surprise awakening us,
the surprise that he loved us first,
so that everything else is response to that first love,
life itself being one long relaxing into the discovery of being loved,
and then one long slow learning of how to mirror that love of his.

If faith between you brings you together today,
faith beyond you brings you together here in God's house;
both kinds of faith are born from surprise at being loved at all.

From love is born faith; from faith is born hope.
Today your hope gives birth to a great decision,
a decision to risk the surprises of life together.

That risk is rooted in trust, not only in one another,
but in someone beyond you
Who is also someone with you and within you.
Someone who says, 'I am love.
I show my love in Jesus so that you might have life.
I loved you first and so you can have the same love for one another.
If you love one another, my love lives on in you
and will come to fullness in You.'

Michael Paul Gallagher SJ

2

Hope

The mountains and the sea

Readings: Prov 3:3-10. Ps 28. 71.

The mountains and the sea, the visible and concrete heights, and the invisible and abstract depths, conjure up over and over again the words of many psalms:

> The Lord's voice resounding on the waters,
> the Lord on the immensity of the waters. (Ps 28:3)

> May the mountains bring forth peace for the people
> and the hills, justice. (Ps 71:3)

The mountains portray all the obstacles in life, the many difficulties and dangers. They are almost terrifying and forbidding, something to be avoided or skirted. Yet, anyone who has ever climbed a high mountain will realise that it presents more of a *challenge* than a difficulty. There is always the other side of the mountain, and then the exhilaration of having conquered and triumphed over a material obstacle. This is also true of marriage. It is a challenge, demanding effort and sacrifice. It is very much a setting out into the unknown, uncharted path of life. In marriage, it is not one person, facing the unknown alone, but two people, two as one, who will be making the effort together. Their combined strength and spirit will help them face all the challenges of life.

And then there is the sea, a symbol of the immensity of God's creation, but also a symbol of *freedom* and *eternity*. So many strange and wonderful fish living there, so much life, and mysterious life, in the depths.

> Out of the depths I cry to you, O Lord,
> Lord, hear my voice. (Ps 129:1-2)

The sea conveys a reassuring message that there is no emptiness in this world and above all that there is no emptiness, no nothingness in the other world. The endless lapping of the waves on the shore, the echo of some real noise in the hollow sea-shell, the sheer vastness of it all, is an image of something and someone greater than ourselves. God is in the ocean, as he is on the mountain.

As you both go through life, you will gather together many things, many possessions, and you will reap much fruit. You are about to form a family, as well as to set up a home. Your family and your home will need a sure foundation, the solid base of *wisdom*. That wisdom is to be found in God and in the contemplation of God's creation. It is expressed in the sigh of wonder and the cry of joy in being part of a mysterious world. Keep on wondering, keep on crying out in joy, and in your days of happiness and of sorrow, seek out the mountains and the sea. They will speak words of wisdom to you, straight from the mouth and mind of God.

Mark Tierney OSB

Don't be afraid

Readings: Gen 2:18-24. Ps 127. I Jn 4:1-7

Alleluia, alleluia.
As long as we love one another
God will live in us,
And his love will be complete in us.
Alleluia.

I. . . take you. . . for better, for worse, for richer, for poorer, in sickness and in health, all the days of our life.

There is hope for us all when men and women can say these words to each other. They express trust in the present and hope for the future. In fact, when you come to think of it, we have to take love on trust. And the only way to face the future is with hope in our hearts.

There is always an element of risk in making decisions about the future. There is the fear of failure and only a fool has no fear. The fact of the matter is that our own resources are inadequate when it comes to the hope of a love that abides forever. That is why it is such a comfort to hear our Lord's words: 'What *God* joins together man must not separate. . .' So when fear gnaws at us we face our fear with our faith. We listen to Our Lord saying: 'Don't be afraid. I am with you always.'

Our Lord is with us in marriage in a very special way. When a couple accept each other as man and wife they signify the love of Christ for all of us. Their acceptance of each other is a sign of his love just as surely as the bread and wine after the words of consecration signify the reality of the presence of Christ in our midst. So, do not be afraid.

The only moment that we can grasp is this present moment. The past is gone and the future is yet to be. But the future is shaped by the decisions that we make today. The future grows out of the present. We rejoice with this couple at this present moment and we share their hope for the future.

Henry Peel OP

Joy and hope

Readings: 1 Cor 12:13–13:8. Jn 15:9-12

We share the joy of a couple in their love for each other and we share their hopes as they take this step on the road of life together.

In this marriage ceremony, we are aware of the deepest reason for that joy. A couple's love shows us something of the reality of God. The love of husband and wife is the first image of God that we find in the Bible: 'In the image of God he created him, male and female he created them.' When they try to express the meaning of their love, they will use words which belong first and foremost to God, words like faithful, generous, everlasting, life-giving. In this wedding Mass, we thank God for what he is and for what he shows us of himself in the love a couple.

They are setting out on a road which will have its potholes and its steep climbs and its occasional collisions. They set out with hope because they know that love can bear all things, hope all things, endure all things.

Love is a task, the task set out in the reading – to be patient and kind, not envious or self seeking. A wise priest used to say to a couple who came to be married, 'You know, this marriage *won't* work!' The point he was making was that every marriage has to be *made* to work. In fact, they will only see the strength of their love for each other when they see what it costs in effort, in generosity, in forgiveness and in understanding. Love grows only in overcoming selfishness.

They do not set out on the road alone. That is the meaning of our presence here with them, people who love them and who will be with them. They are setting out to be a sign of joy and hope, of the life-giving power of love. They can show that in their own home, in the way they enrich one another and the children the Lord may send them; they can show that in their relationship with us, their families and friends and in the way they enrich the whole community to which they belong.

We pray that they may have a marriage that fills their home and all around them with the love that never fails and that they may always know the fulfillment of Christ's promise, that his joy may be in them and that their joy may be full.

+ Donal Murray

The blind leap

Readings: Ps 27:13-14. 1 Cor 13:4-8

A child takes its first few faltering steps. Parents watch excitedly, anxiously, hopefully; hands outstretched to catch him if he falls. And fall he does. But the process is irreversible. Other steps follow. Childhood is signposted with firsts. First day at school. Mother holds his hand as he tearfully and fearfully leaves the cosiness of home and mother's love for the tougher noisy world of classroom and playground. First Communion launches him in another world, the sacramental and the sacred. Centre-stage again, he revels in the limelight, the adulation of aunts, the photographs and the presents. The years pass, each bringing its own firsts as he nervously makes his way through adolescence. First dance, first love, first job, first flat. Rites of passage, pilgrim's progress, steps along a road never to be travelled again. Each step into the unknown. Each step in hope. In fact, hope, as Karl Barth so succinctly put it, is 'just taking the next step'.

The next step is marriage. Paths cross. Love blossoms. Engagement follows. Each walks up the aisle alone, the last steps of a separate existence. Arm-in-arm they come down the aisle stepping out together into the future. Love comes before and hopefully, love will come after too, but marriage itself is a colossal act of hope. And not without risk.

> Hope without risk
> is not hope,
> which is believing
> in risky loving,
> trusting others
> in the dark,
> the blind leap,
> letting God take over. *Helder Camara*

The blind leap, risky loving, for better or for worse.

The cycle continues. First home. First night. First child. First row. And every one of them a sign of hope. Hope carries us from the first tottering steps of the faltering child to the last faltering steps of old age, tottering on the brink of eternity. Hope is each step of each path of life, converging on the aisle of this church today. Some call it destiny. Believers call it God. Marriages are made in heaven.

Hope brought you up this aisle today, to exchange vows. Hope will give you the courage to walk down the aisle together into the sunlight and the future. 'The future,' as Vatican II observed, 'is in the hands of those who know how to give tomorrow's generations reasons to live and hope.' In your hands.

> This I believe: I shall see the goodness of God
> in the land of the living.
> Put your hope in God, be strong, let your heart be bold.
> Put your hope in God. (Ps 27:13-14)

Liam Swords

Things that matter

Readings: Eph 5:1-20. 1 Pet 3:1-13.

You can do no greater honour to a person than to trust him. When in our worship we say, I believe in God, we do not say only that we know God exists, we say also that we accept him and believe what he says.

We are often reminded that men and women are made in the image of God. Our response has sometimes been, 'Very well then, let us think how God could possibly be like us.' What we should say is, 'Let us think how like him we are.' When our friends turn to each other in love and say they accept each other they are saying, 'This good friend at my side has godlike qualities, able to love, able to share and create life, able to inspire trust and to be trusted.'

Our future life, on this earth and after it, is founded on hope; on the hope which our closest friends inspire in us; on the hope that such love for each other is deep enough and strong enough and sympathetic enough to last for ever.

We cannot demand absolute assurances here and now that all will be well and that our love for each other will last all our earthly lives. We cannot demand of our marriage partner now that in every possible set of circumstances in the future he or she will be able and willing to give us the assurance, the happiness and support we need and hope for. There are times when even the best falter. But because we love we hope. Because we hope, we love.

We are glad to remember that our Lord had a lesson for this too. He could have arranged events in such a way that not one of his closest friends would have let him down. He did not do that. He could have contrived things in such a way that Joseph would never have doubted Mary for an instant. But he did not. We would have been glad if he had not told Mary he was unwilling to do what she asked – at a wedding party too – or sent out word one day that he was too busy to see her. But he had his own way of telling us about things that matter and here he was saying that the sweetness of every friendship is enhanced, not destroyed, by the momentary bitterness, refusal or anger. What is important is the trust, the hope, which we have in each other's good will. The breaking down of the fences is not a disaster if we have thought about, prayed about and practised the craft of mending them.

Forgiveness is easy if you have hope. Forgiveness, like hope, has to do with the future. When we disagree or feel anger towards each

33

other it may seem as if love has drained away from us disastrously. It has not. Forgiveness recreates it, gives new life to it, draws us to each other more firmly than ever.

For this we need to allow God's peace and good will, his forgiveness and renewal to penetrate our minds, to surrender at least a little of our sovereignty to God and to each other.

It is only a hopeful person who can forgive and love like that.

Desmond Wilson

New wine for old

Readings: Jer 31:31-34. Rom 12:1-2, 9-13. Jn 2:1-11

A wedding is a time of joy and celebration. It is full of the confidence of new beginnings. Both of you come to this altar as different individuals, from different families, with different life experiences. Thus far you have sought to develop your lives as individuals, faithful to God's commandments, seeking out his will for you, trying to be faithful to your baptismal calling to be followers of Christ. Now, however, you seek to join your lives together in such a fashion that the two of you will become as one.

You have been blessed by a friendship that has brought you to this altar. You have grown in your knowledge of one another, your love for each other has matured, no doubt, through the various experiences of your courtship. Perhaps you have been led through the opportunity of marriage preparation to gain valuable insights into the sacrament of marriage which you are about to enter.

Yet the future for which your prepare yourselves is hidden from you. The instruction for the old nuptial mass said it beautifully:

> You are about to enter into a union which is most sacred and most serious. It is most sacred because established by God himself; most serious, because it will bind you together in a relationship so close and so intimate, that it will profoundly influence your whole future. That future, with its hopes and disappointments, its successes and it failures, its pleasures and its pains, its joys and its sorrows, is hidden from your eyes.

And so you stand before us to pronounce mutual vows of life-long love and fidelity and take one another in good times and in bad, in sickness and in health, all the days of your life. I see in the miracle of the wedding at Cana a beautiful symbol of Christ's presence and powerful love in your lives.

In the narrative we are told that at one point in the wedding reception the wine ran out. Jesus, after Mary's request to do something about this embarrassment, instructed the waiters to fill six stone water jars with water and take them to the chief steward. To his great amazement he noted that the best wine had been saved until last!

This is a great and wonderful day for you. Some people say this will be the best year of your lives. I don't believe it. If that were true, it would all be downhill from here. I believe you are entering into a partnership of love which is a marvellous journey with Christ. In every journey, there are trials and difficulties which must be overcome. I believe that it is the nature of love to meet these difficulties and overcome these challenges. But as Christians we know that cannot happen without the help of the Lord.

I see in those six stone water jars a symbol of ourselves in our humanity. At the beginning of our journey we are confident, secure, full of the anticipation of success that characterises youth. But as we go along in our journey, we empty ourselves in those worthwhile endeavours of life that call us forth. There comes a point where we realise that we have nothing more to give. This point of realisation might come gradually or of a sudden, sooner rather than later. It is a realisation that as the scripture says 'without Christ we can do nothing'.

It is at this point in our journey that we turn to Christ in a new way. We ask him to fill us with his love, his strength, his guidance. We seek to be taught the way of self-giving love that he so powerfully exemplified in his life. Then in our own emptiness we are filled with a beautiful gift of life and love that comes to us from the very source of life and love. It is that wine of life that all recognised as the best that was saved until last.

You are about to enter onto a journey in which this wonderful moment, great as it is, is not going to be your finest. Nor will this first year of marriage, great as it is, be your best. I wish for you rather a long life together. A life in which you come to know the meaning and the power of love as Christ has taught – self-emptying love. May you come to know, through the struggle that comes with dying to yourself in order to live for others, the better wine that is Christ. May Christ be with you in all things teaching you the power of love that shows itself in a generous measure of acceptance, in forgiveness, in mutual respect, generosity, unselfish service of others and a joyful spirit as Paul so beautifully describes these deeds of love in his letter to the Romans.

Robert Rivers CSP

From small beginnings

Reading: Mt 13:31-32, 44

Those two stories are being re-written by our two friends here. The parables of Jesus are traps to invite us to wonder about life and here we can wonder about what this couple are about to offer in hope to one another. Why are they doing it? How can they dare do it! The stories give us a glimpse of an answer.

The second story is what has already happened and what we pray will continue to happen for this couple. It's a story of discovery of something rich and deep in the field, something that makes one want to let go of everything else in order to own that field, something that causes a huge happiness. This couple would not be here today if they did not know the experience of that story in their own way. . .

The other story is about something slow and almost unperceivable, a growth that takes years, from small beginning to a great tree where branches give shelter. That's the story of trusting, daring, hoping which this couple will re-write in ways unknown to us now. That's the story of the future, just as the hidden treasure is partly already discovered. . .

All of the stories of Jesus are about ordinary things, human things, but they are stories about us and God. So our prayer is that this couple may find him too through the adventure of their own humanity. He is the hidden treasure. He is the secret source of the growth of that tree. He is not always noticed: faith is not always out in the open. But through the loving of the years, faith can be found. Perhaps the way to God in marriage is through one another and through that tree and its branches as it grows to giving generous shelter for others. . .

Michael Paul Gallagher

3
Fidelity

High fidelity

Readings: Eph 5:22-33. 1 Cor 13:4-7. Gal 5:9-22

When the Jews wished to describe the faithful love God has for his people they chose the imagery of a husband remaining faithful to his erring wife, waiting in love and patience for her return to him. This image emphasises an aspect of fidelity that we tend to overlook; for faithfulness means not only keeping your own side of the bargain but also believing that your partner will keep their's – someday! – even when, and maybe especially when, the behaviour of that spouse gives you very little grounds for so believing.

Marriage is never more truly a sacrament of God's love than when the going gets tough. Just as we do not see the growth that starts at baptism until the child itself has done a lot of growing, we don't notice the true growth of the sacrament of matrimony until the honeymoon period is over and the partners start growing together. Growing involves change, adjustment and usually some discomfort, as parents of any teething baby will tell you, but it is then that the virtue of faithfulness begins to develop. This should come as no surprise, for Jesus has told us, 'If you love those who love you what right have you to claim any credit?' (Mt 5) and there are times in any marriage when loving your spouse seems every bit as difficult as loving your enemy. It is in times like these that the grace of fidelity will give you the strength to be 'always ready to excuse, to trust, to hope and to endure whatever comes' (1 Cor 13:7).

Infidelity does not necessarily mean adultery; that is just one of its most extreme expressions. There are other more subtle and much more common ways that can undermine faithfulness to each other, like running home to mother to complain of his or her little faults and failings, criticising your partner behind backs, being sceptical and unsupportive towards attempts at improvement. A negative and disloyal attitude like that can poison married love.

What a glorious and comforting thing it is to have a faithful and loyal companion on the tough road through life; to know that whatever life may throw at you there is one person who is truly on your side, who will champion your cause, take your part and accept your version of the story; someone who will sympathise with your disappointments and enjoy your triumphs even more than you do yourself!

When this has been done for so long that fidelity has become second nature, and you're as unlikely to be untrue to your spouse as to be untrue to yourself, then Christian marriage becomes the great sign, that St Paul talks about, of the love of Christ for his beloved bride, the Church.

Cathal & Norah O Boyle

The gold standard

Reading: Gen 9:8-17

In the geriatric unit of a hospital the old women sat blanketed against the cold and the busy world around them. Between half sentences of confusion they would lapse into silence and begin to examine their old withered, worked hands and would focus in on their wedding rings and circle them on bony, brittle fingers. How many documentary films were in this ward? Here were stories of love promised and promises kept in days of grinding poverty and occasional sun shafts of joy. They had experienced many things richer than money and many things poorer than the lack of it.

The ring twirling on the finger was the sign of that promise. God used a rainbow when he made a pact with Noah. Is it still a sign in the evening sky that he will not flood the world with water or nuclear fallout? Will he prevent the trickle of blood in today's killings from becoming the bloodbath of pogroms or isolated wars? Maybe today's world knows the theory of light refraction and rainbows lose their meaning!

Surely this ring of marriage hasn't lost it meaning in an age that would only measure by the gold standard and world prices. Its value can certainly be measured but not the price.

Some people see life today as a wilderness and the temptation to end life-long commitments are many. With so much uncertainty, with a future not guaranteeed in nuclear nervousness can anyone say forever? Diamonds are forever, as we're told, then so is gold and so can be the unbroken circle it symbolises in the wedding ring.

Today at this altar you say with grace and courage that you will share life in good days and bad as long as life lasts. We, your friends, will be with you because your love and happiness gives all of us new hope, a lighter step, a surer path in our pilgrim way to God. Perhaps, today, as we celebrate with you, we might think again that the ultimate sign of God's never ending love for us was in the shape of a cross and a son hanging there in no-man's land between heaven and earth. Then it may begin to dawn on us, creatures for a day, that pain and love were twins on Calvary and that, wherever there was deep love since, the gold and the ashes were never far apart.

John J McCullagh

Faithfulness

Reading: 1 Cor 13:4-7

True friends take each other for granted – in the good sense of that phrase. They take it that they will always be there for each other. They do not subject their friendship to continuous analysis or exploratory operation. For them, being faithful is no longer a duty. It reflects what they have become. One would as soon deceive oneself as deceive the other. They live for each other but do not make any song and dance about it. For them this is their life. It all seems so easy – until you back track. You soon discover how long a climb it took to reach this plateau. Nothing worthwhile comes in life or love without personal effort. The effort is the secret. The marriage ceremony is no magic wand. Neither is the sacrament. Grace is no escalator. It just provides energy for the climb.

The trajectory of that climb is a constant upward curve. There are squiggles marking differences and dips showing backslides. But a row never heralds the absence of true love. One only really differs with someone, and seriously differs, when one cares enough about him or her and about one's relationship. In mere acquaintanceship convention allows one to pass on painlessly to the next item on the agenda.

'Love is patient, love is kind. . . forgives all things, bears all things' (1 Cor 13:47). If love were an easy option there would be no need of a commandment. At the romantic stage it is as easy as the phrase 'falling into' suggests. Growing it on to maturity, to the stage when it is taken for granted, is a costly process in terms of the generous, patient, thoughtful and forgiving spirit which it demands.

Faithfulness is not a matter of avoiding infidelity. It is caring for another as for oneself. When both feel this way about each other love has a home. When one only remains true to a pledged love married virtue is indeed heroic. It reflects God's own faithfulness who remains loyal to his covenant of love in spite of human neglect and betrayal.

Most marriages fall between the extremes. The mature honest couple will lose little time on recrimination about who is to blame for these past common or garden failings which beset every human enterprise. They will get down to building a better and happier future for them both. As the old Irish proverb has it: The common sense bought by experience is worth double commonsense at second hand.

Denis O'Callaghan

The Lord be with you

Readings: Ruth 1:15-18. Tobit 14:8, 10-11. Prov 5:15, 18-19

There is as good fish in the sea as ever came out of it. The resources of the human spirit are as fruitfully creative today as ever they were. God's readiness to help his people has not diminished.

The desire of the human heart to make of life something beautiful for God and for one another is deeply rooted in our being. That it is not good for man to be alone is demonstrated by the prevalence of the modern scourge of loneliness.

Communications are the success story of this generation. Relationships, however, which should thrive on the unlimited possibilities of the electronic media, do not flourish as they should.

Marriage is a bridge to self-discovery and maturation. We take our lives into our hands and entrust them into the hands of another whom we love, trust and totally accept. Trust springs from the generosity of one heart reaching out to another. Love is always learning, is always an apprentice.

To be loved is no less important than to be fed. To be somebody for others, at least for another, is a powerful affirmation. To be all things to a spouse is not a limitation but a liberation from selfishness, the prime enemy. Through our giving in love nothing is lost; all is gain. A union of hearts makes it possible for a couple to be open to the whole human race, to become the warm centre of a whole neighbourhood.

Fidelity is basic to good relationships. Fickleness is a quagmire. God is faithful, rock, truth. God prizes fidelity in his people. Fidelity is the core quality of marriage. The total fidelity of the God of Abraham, Isaac, Jacob and Joseph is the model for true marriage. God cannot forget his people. Their names are written on the palm of his hand. The true Israelite took his cue from the Torah, 'It is not good that man should be alone. I will make him a helpmate,' (Gen 2:18) and found in the book of Tobit an ideal nourished by prayer and faith. 'And now my child, I lay this duty on you: serve God sincerely, and do what is pleasing to him. And lay on your children the obligation to behave uprightly, to give alms, to keep God in mind and to bless his name always, sincerely and with all their might. . .' (Tobit 14:8, 10-11).

Where love and friendship dwell, there is God in their midst. The coinage of love must not be debased. Songs of love fill the air but what is the quality of the love they celebrate? We purify our

43

understanding of love by reference to its source in the wisdom of God mediated to us through Jesus Christ. God is love, unadulterated and totally beneficent. True wisdom, holy wisdom as celebrated in scripture, is compared with the faithful wife, spouse, husband to be sure. Betrayal (= adultery) is folly, the negation of what God wills.

Drink the water from your own cistern,
fresh water from your own well. . .
Find joy with the wife you married in your youth,
fair as a hind, graceful as a fawn.
Let hers be the company you keep. . .
Hers the love that ever holds you captive. (Prov 5:15, 18-19)

P J Brophy

As I have loved you

Readings: 1 Cor 13. Jn 15:11-17

Those words of Jesus at the Last Supper come alive for us in a special way here, not as words from the past but as promises in the present. They speak of four realities that seem huge and abstract: joy and love, self-giving and choosing. But today it is the couple who give reality to those realities for us. Today it is you who help us to hear those words of Jesus sounding in your present tense. You are here to offer promises to one another, promises about joy and love, self-giving and choosing. The rest of us are here because we believe in what you are doing.

But we are all here in this Church and around this altar because of another reason, because our lives can reach out for another horizon, the horizon of God. Let us listen to those simple words of Jesus while watching the stained glass window of you two about to be married here. If my joy can be in you, he says, your human joy together will be full, full-filled. If you think of yourselves only as my distant servants, you will never know my heart; just as if you stayed distant from one another, you would never have found the friendship that expanded into this moment now. I too want to be with you in friendship and then you will know me differently. You come to promise love, but what is that really? The love I speak of is not simply love-one-another but love as I have loved you. I had to lay down my life for my friends. So will you. The surrender you promise today will cost something with the years. That is what you mean in the rich and realist words you are about to speak to one another: taking each other for life, hoping of course for better but willing to share worse, facing richer or poorer, sickness and health. We heard St Paul speaking in vast terms of love as the only eternal survivor of God's gifts here, but in the same breath he speaks of love as very everyday, the overcoming of envies and prides. So too we are about to hear you give promises to one another, promises to last for ever. But that 'for ever' will be lived in the adventure of the everyday.

That could be frightening if your promises were not blessed and embraced by the promises of Christ himself. My joy will meet yours. My friendship will crown yours. My choice will bless yours. So love one another, as I have, and as I will continue to do through the everyday into eternity.

Michael Paul Gallagher SJ

A new language

Readings: Jer 31:31-34. Ps 144. 1 Jn 3:18-24

Alleluia, alleluia.
God is love;
let us love one another
as God has loved us.
Alleluia.

'I. . . take you. . . for better, for worse, for richer for poorer, in sickness and in health, all the days of our life.'

We have all heard these words before, I suppose. Many who are now listening have said them to one another. This might well be an occasion for repeating them with a new depth of meaning. After all, the bride and groom are not saying these words now simply so that they can listen to each other. They are saying them publicly for all of us to hear. They are doing something which is significant, not just for themselves, but for the whole Church of God. It brings the love of Christ for all of us into our midst in quite a new way.

So, in a sense, we have never heard these words before. We have never heard them in quite the same way before. We have never heard this couple say them to each other before. This is a unique moment. We might even hear them as a particular application of the inspired word of God: 'Behold I am making all things new'.

When a child learns how to say a new word there is great joy all around. And the child loves to repeat the new word that it has just learned. There is delight in the new discovery. The bride and groom are no longer children except, hopefully, in the profound sense that our Lord meant: 'Unless we become as little children we shall not enter the kingdom of heaven.' When the child within us dies there is no room for growth any more. We have nothing more to learn. Then, indeed, the joy has gone from our lives.

This couple have not just learned a new word. They are beginning to learn a whole new language. This language takes a whole lifetime to learn, but those who persevere assure us that the effort is well worthwhile. Indeed to learn the language of love is the most worthwhile experience of living. It is a pearl beyond price.

This language is just a matter of words. Its most perfect expression is 'The Word was made flesh and dwelt amongst us'. All genuine love is a sharing in that great reality. We are witnessing a great mystery – a sign of the love of Christ for his Church.   *Henry Peel OP*

Unconditional commitment

Readings: Gen 2:18-24. 1 Cor 13. Mt 19:3-6

It is very consoling to know that this great partnership into which you are about to enter is a partnership that was designed by our Creator God from the very beginning. At the heart of God's creation is a love story between a man and a woman. God formed man and woman to be companions, partners in a life-long journey of love. And though that first love story is a love story gone awry, from that moment on there has existed a wonderful institution of marriage which is built upon the partnership of a man and a woman in love. It is that partnership which you seek to form by standing before God, before the community of the Church as you promise mutal vows of life-long love and fidelity to one another in the sacrament of marriage.

Yet you come to that institution of marriage as unique individuals with your own personalities, your own history, your own experience. Out of these two separate and individual lives you seek to make yourselves one by God's grace and the power of his love. And so marriage is a combination of age-old realities, yet something profoundly new because of the fact that it is the two of you who are entering into this mystery.

Let us explore for a moment the wonder of this partnership by looking at the vows which you will shortly pronounce before us. You are about to utter these words: 'I take you to be my wife (husband). I promise to be true to you in good times and in bad, in sickness and in health. I will love you and honour you all the days of my life.' What is first of all striking is that these words speak of unconditional commitment. You are not saying to one another: 'I take you in good times but not bad, as long as someone better does not come along, and I'll love you as long as you love me.' No. Each of you is binding yourself without condition.

When we speak of unconditional commitment and trust, we are really speaking of the heroic dimension of marriage. Now let us speak for a moment of fidelty and permanence which recognise something of the human dimensions of this wonderful journey. Jesus commands us to enter into marriage as a permanent and indissoluble commitment. You are about to promise to one another that this relationship of mutual love is an exclusive one between the two of you. What you seek to build is a partnership of mutual self-giving that is complete and total, and therefore beautifully symbolised in the act of intercourse.

The instruction for the old marriage rite used to applaud the courage and faith of couples in these words: 'It is a beautiful tribute to your undoubted faith in each other that, recognising the full import of these words you are nevertheless so willing and ready to pronounce them.' No couple stands before God and the community of the Church to utter the solemn vows of marriage without a keen awareness of their own weakness and inadequacy. How do we live up to these exalted promises to love one another as God has loved us? Surely one of the important consolations of marriage is that we are entering into a partnership of mutual help, in which we commit ourselves to one another in a way that we will do so with no one else. The fidelity of marriage is a commitment to give each other the space to be human, to grow, to fail as well as succeed, to change without the fear that we will be traded in for another partner. Surely the first meaning of fidelity is that we are committing ourselves to an exclusive relationship of total giving because that is the nature of love – to grow as well as grow old together.

Finally, we speak of permanence. Not only is this an exclusive partnership but it is a partnership in which we commit ourselves to go all the way with each other. Unconditional commitment demands this. The total giving of ourselves in marriage could not tolerate the insecurity of knowing that for whatever reasons one of the partners might one day simply decide to bale out.

This is the partnership into which you are about to enter. It is founded upon your willingness to be faithful to the solemn words you are about to utter. Yet surely one more word needs to be said. The relationship of mutual giving, faithful and enduring to the end is really another word for love. St Paul speaks a word which reveals that the partnership of marriage is not a matter of making a commitment and living our lives in a kind of endurance contest. The commitment of marriage is a journey in which we seek to grow in love.

May your lives be filled with enduring love and joy.

Robert Rivers CSP

Until death do us part

Reading: Jn 17:20-26

It was an Autumn evening when the whole world seemed to weep. Soggy leaves littered the footpath as I made my way to the church. The rain was penetrating, the wind cold.

As I entered the church it was difficult even to see the altar in the gathering dusk. I knelt in the last pew.

I thought the church was empty. Then I heard deep throbbing sobs coming from the front of the building. As my eyes became accustomed to the twilight I discerned a very small, pathetic bundle of a figure, way ahead of me.

I went up to comfort the sorrowing person. It was a little old man. On enquiring the cause of such grief, he replied sobbing 'My wife died six months ago and I am heart broken. I don't know how to live without her.' The man, whose name was Sean, told me that he was eighty years of age.

In concluding the conversation Sean said, 'All I now want to do is to die, to be with her.'

This is a true story. It was on that day that I became convinced that love can grow and fidelity is possible.

In the face of a society that encourages everyone to pursue individualism, Jesus calls his people to unity, even to perfect unity. The fidelity of husband and wife is a sign of God's unbroken covenant love for his people.

Martin Tierney

I will

Readings: 1 Cor 7:10-16, 13:1-13. Gal 5:13-26

The Duchess of Plaza Toro, in the Gilbert and Sullivan opera *The Gondoliers*, in giving marital advice to her daughter, claims that loving one's husband is only a question of determination. 'I loved your father,' she says. 'It was very difficult, my dear, but I said to myself, "That man is a Duke and I *will* love him." Several of my relations bet me I couldn't but I did – desperately!' Well, her motive may be rather mercenary and her attitude comical, but there is a grain of truth in what she says.

The *reasons* usually given for the breakdown of marriage do not necessarily actually *cause* any marriage to break down. Shortage of money, ill health, alcoholism, even adultery do not inevitably mean that a partnership will break up, even though they put it under great strain. There are homes where there is very little money and a lot of happiness, other homes where one spouse cares for a handicapped or ailing partner with love and devotion through years of ill health, not only without complaint but with joy; marriages where one supports the other in the long struggle for sobriety, and even marriages where an adulterous spouse has been forgiven and been welcomed back and the relationship has been healed and strengthened by love.

There are marriages where everything seemed to promise that they would live happily ever after, which seemed to have everything going for them, similar backgrounds, good jobs, a comfortable home, good looks and a pleasant disposition and still the marriage has not lasted.

So what is the magic ingredient? The Duchess has put her finger on one of the essentials and that is will power or determination, not always like her grim determination, but none the less determination to make marriage work. In the marriage rite it is called 'consent'. Consent on the wedding day is not the whole of the story. That consent, once freely given, cannot be cancelled but politicians are not the only ones who do not always fulfil their promises and in fact couples will give their consent to marriage every day of their married lives. When that determination weakens and the consent is no longer practised, marriage will inevitably breakdown.

To make sure that the will to stay married remains strong and secure, place your marriage today under the guidance and protection of the Holy Spirit. He will give you the power and courage necessary to be the sign in this world of what the Spirit of love is. Just as human parenthood can help us to realise the creative care of God the Father, and the Incarnation brings us close to God the Son, so the special calling of married people is to be the image and likeness on earth of the Spirit of love. When we see two people who cannot bear to be separated, whose greatest joy is to be together, whose love is generous and creative, then we begin to realise that the Holy Spirt of love is no vague, shadowy, ghostly being but the vibrant, creative force that makes not only the world but even the universe go round.

Cathal & Norah O Boyle

4

One-ness

Thanks for everything

Readings: Col 3:12-17. Jn 17:20-23

At a wedding we are the privileged witnesses of a historical moment. We make history everyday but we don't make recorded history everyday. But in a few moments from now when this couple give and receive each other in marriage they will make recorded history and we are happy to be present, and part of history in the making.

We are living witnesses to their love and gift. But it will be recorded officially too. Names will go in a book announcing to generations yet unborn that this moment took place. Perhaps 200 years from now someone with a name we couldn't pronounce from some odd corner of the world may come here looking for ancestors, looking in the parish register, saying, 'I think my great great grandparents were married here around the end of the twentieth century, ah! look! there it is!' And they'll be pleased to find you, as we your friends are happy that you found each other.

So this marriage is historical, but it has an importance beyond that. Some day there will be no witness left, some day the writing will fade. But what happens here becomes in a way immortal. The words spoken may be quiet words but they will flow on through time and go beyond that to ripple into eternity.

At this moment God breaks through the dust of the everyday and the ordinary and marks two people as his and marks this moment as part of the everlasting covenant. Just as they become each other's and promise in the words of Ruth that 'your people will be my people', God promises that they shall be his people and he their God, to protect and help and cherish them.

So marriage is a moment of new communion – communion between themselves and communion between them and God. And we all give thanks for that and we give thanks that you have gathered us into your communion – because your first gift to us all is that you have brought us together. This moment of marriage is a eucharistic moment for us all – covenant, communion and thanksgiving.

For the couple, the celebrants of the sacrament, it is a very personal

53

eucharist. They give thanks for each other – for if one didn't exist the other could not be so happy. And even more than that, in a way they are like the bread and wine that are changed in the Mass. That bread and that wine began their mysterious journeys far apart and separately – the wine in a vineyard in Spain maybe, the bread in a wheatfield in Canada perhaps. And through one chance after another they have finally reached this altar together, to be changed into the one body of Christ.

They, like the bread and wine, have come a long journey of days, a long journey of acquaintance, from being apart and totally unaware of each other to meeting, to knowing, to loving and to this moment of being changed at this altar into husband and wife, in the communion of life. And as at the first Eucharist they have gathered their friends about them to celebrate the gift and union of their lives.

So here were are – friends and God – hanging on their words. We stand round them like a chorus wishing them well, singing their praises, and hoping for all that is good for them. And we pray that every Mass they ever attend will remind them of this day. And whatever comes their way, may they have each other to give thanks for at every Eucharist.

Thomas Waldron

Not good to be alone

Reading: Gen 1:26-31

All religions have their stories about God, mankind and the world. The Bible is our name for the Jewish-Christian story which shapes our thoughts and feelings about the mystery of life. The very first pages of the story of creation places man as the crown of creation, at the highest level of the scale of life, in charge of the world around him and outside of that, the sun, moon and stars and the expanse of the mysterious universe. But inside man lies the mysterious world of human nature, the mystery of the human person as man and woman. That human person, the image and likeness of God, is both male and female.

So we read that 'It is not good for the human person to be alone.' The individual person cannot exist as male or female without the other. To try to do so is to be incomplete. 'It is not good to be alone' holds for human living in general. Man and woman need each other for human life in their joint contribution to building each other as persons and their joint task of building the world. 'It is not good to be alone' is particularly true of the relationship of man and woman as husband and wife.

'My other half' is our way of saying what is meant to happen, a simple phrase for expressing a profound truth. It tells of the growing contentment, closeness and support of the other's presence, of the sense of having the other within as part of oneself. It flows from the experience of a two-way loving which unites husband and wife as a couple and expands them as individuals. He helps her to become a woman; she helps him to become a man. Every man and woman is both male and female and in every person the inner marriage of the masculine and feminine qualities is to take place. Through her he can find the hidden feminine part of himself; through him she can find the hidden masculine part of herself. So in being husband and wife to each other, man and woman fulfil each other, complete each other in their shared life and love.

At this stage of human history it is now becoming possible for men and women to join together in the task of becoming fully human by relating at a deeper level. The renewal of attitudes to one another promises a richer partnership of the spirit than has been seen up to now.

Knowing in their hearts that it is not good for them to be alone the bridegroom and bride each become husband and wife. So in

finding themselves through each other they will know it is good for
them to be together.

Tony Baggot SJ

Needing each other

Readings: Gen 2:18-24. Eph 5:21-23

Through relationship with others we grow as persons. The relationship between man and woman is a unique relationship. The one brings out the best in the other.

Marriage is a beginning. But marriage is also discovering. People grow tired of everything in life. Fashions are always changing. People grow tired of styles in clothes, in houses, in transport, but man and woman never grow tired of discovering one another. It was so from the very beginning when Adam discovered Eve. The awakening of man to the love of a woman is one of the most beautiful things there is in life. And the marvellous thing is that man and woman in marriage go on discovering each other, go on discovering new depths in each other, new sources of joy and surprise, new riches. Man and woman need each other. They belong to each other. 'It is not good for man to be alone.'

Marriage is beginning, discovering, but it is also adjusting and this is one of the most delicate aspects of marriage. As soon as the din of the wedding bells has died down, as soon as the excitement of the honeymoon is over, the young couple begin to discover cracks and weaknesses in one another that they never suspected. But if they can make allowances, if they can exercise patience during this critical period of their lives, if they can adjust to one another, the chances are that the rest of their married existence will be plain sailing.

Marriage is beginning, discovering, adjusting. Marriage is also sharing. It is the deepest sharing there can be in life. As the Second Vatican Council puts it, 'a sharing of life and of love'. A sharing of their very persons. They become not merely two in one flesh, but two in one life. The more closely united they are to one another, the more does the husband become himself, the more does the wife become herself. Union does not destroy. The closer the union, the more do they grow as persons.

And finally, marriage is revealing. It reveals the self-giving love of Christ, for it is the sacrament of Christ's love for his Church and of the Church's fidelity to Christ.

Eltin Griffin OCarm

Peeling the onion

Reading: Eph 4:1-6, 14-16

I met Peter the other day. He was a real good friend during my schooldays. We began reminiscing. 'Where is Austin now?' he asked. 'I think he went to Australia,' I replied. I added as an afterthought, 'To be honest, it is years since I heard from him, perhaps he is dead.' Austin was the third partner in our youthful triumvirate.

Austin had gone to the University in another city. In the beginning, we saw him during holiday time. Then the odd letter. Finally silence. We had ceased to communicate. As far as we were now concerned, he could be dead.

Communicaiion is the vehicle through which married partners grow in unity. Regular communication in itself serves as a way of seeking that unity 'which has the Spirit as its origin' (Eph. 4:3).

Just as Austin died for Peter and myself because we had ceased to communicate, love also dies, sometimes slowly, when married partners fail to build their unity through regular communication.

Jesus is called the 'Word of God' or the "Word made flesh'. A word is spoken, communicated. God is very much in the communications business. He came to communicate his love, and in turn, he sent his disciples out to 'preach and to heal', to continue the process of communication.

Communication in marriage may be a little like peeling an onion. It's hard at times. It may even make you cry. But it is only when layer after layer of the brown outer skin is peeled away that the real onion appears. And that's nice. Unless we persevere we can never get to the real juicy edible onion.

There are many ways of building unity in marriage, acts of tenderness, sexual intercourse, common interests and activities shared together. However. without communication from the heart, the marriage will never reach its full potential.

Martin Tierney

Matter o' money

Readings: Col 3:1-14. Acts 2:42-47. 1 John 3:13, 16-24

From ancient times in Ireland up to about a hundred years ago, marriage was very much a matter of money. Marriages were very carefully arranged, not so much according to the inclinations of the couple involved but with a view to the most advantageous deal in land or property. It was regarded as much more important that the farms marched together than that the couple had met and felt they could march together through life. The modern idea that they should have 'fallen in love' would have been regarded as dangerous romantic nonsense and no foundation on which to base the serious business of matrimony.

Today the pendulum has swung to the other extreme and it is regarded as slightly indecent to bring up the subject of money on a wedding day. But sooner or later it is a subject that will arise in marriage and differing attitudes and expectations in a husband and wife can be the cause of much heartache and tension.

When employers once tried to avoid payroll robberies by sending the paycheques home, the scheme had to be abandoned because the unions would not agree as their members did not want their wives to find out what they really earned! If the story is true, it is a sad reflection on the state of mistrust existing in some marriages today. A partnership where one partner thinks the other is not to be trusted in a matter of money is off to a very shaky start.

Even where there is trust and openness between a husband and wife about money their priorities and attitudes towards it can be very different. Since we generally absorb these attitudes, like our moral values, from our parents, almost unconsciously, it can take a very long time to readjust.

This might seem a very materialistic approach to a sacrament but it can involve a clash of moral values which is very difficult to resolve. If one thinks that justice demands that all bills be paid promptly and the other believes that giving to charity is more important or more urgent and there is not enough money to do both then, to quote the *Mikado*, 'A is right and B is right and everyone is right as right can be' but some adjustment is essential for marital harmony.

In former days the matchmaker drew up the arrangements about dowries and settlements before the marriage took place, mainly in the interests of the wife for after marriage the man usually had the final say in all financial arrangements. But in these days of great

59

equality and financial partnership if this topic is not explored before marriage – and it rarely is – then there will have to be compromises and adjustments made afterwards. Instead of ignoring this or avoiding it as an uncomfortable or embarrassing area it can be the opportunity for great spiritual growth.

Both of you will need to practise unselfishness and honesty towards each other. Justice, generosity and charity will be needed if your home is to become a Christian community like that described in the Acts of the Apostles where 'All the believers were together and had everything in common. Selling their possessions and goods, they gave to anyone as he had need' (Acts 2:44-45). In this way your home will be a model of the Christian community radiating God's love and generosity to a selfish, materialistic world, and showing that spiritual riches are far more precious and lasting than all the riches or wedding presents of the world. The Spirit of Love is the best wedding gift God could give you today.

Cathal & Norah O Boyle

Mortgage on life

Reading: Song of Songs 8:6-8

'I take you as my husband.' 'I take you as my wife.' Words come easy on the wedding day. Life will spell out the implications. Behind those words is a statement of intent well expressed in the Irish Bishops' Pastoral *Love is for Life:*

> I want you to share your life and your world with me. I want us to build a new life together, a future together, which will be our future. I need you. I can't live without you. I need you to love me, and to love me not just now but always. I will be faithful to you not just now but always. I will never let you down or walk out on you. I will never put anyone else in place of you. I will stay with you through thick and thin. I will be responsible for you and I want you to be responsible for me, no matter what happens.

Marriage is a blank cheque, a mortgage on life. Two people decide to make a home together and commit themselves to whatever it takes. They do not know what is ahead for them. The cynic might say that if they did, they would think again! But that's why the cynic ploughs his lonely furrow.

Two lives do weld into one in the marriages we see, and take for granted. A couple come to know each other as they know themselves. Even in physical appearance they become like one another. Communication is often communing without words. Our cynic may say that if you see a man and woman eating in silence chances are they are married! One sometimes talks a lot when one is unsure of oneself or when one is uncomfortable with someone else.

The Gospel is not only about life hereafter. It is about happiness in day-to-day living. That Gospel draws two people together, while respecting individual dignity and freedom. It deepens love's generosity and keeps jealousy at arms length. At first sight jealousy may present as proof of the oneness which love pledges but it is the worm in the bud. The old Irish poem puts it well:

> Love like heat and cold
> Pierces and then is gone;
> Jealousy when it strikes
> Sticks in the marrowbone.

For the Christian couple this growing into oneness is a Gospel imperative: 'That they may be one as we are one, you Father in me and I in you.' Christ through his spirit cements this union: 'Where two or three are gathered in my name there am I in the midst of them.' If each partner strives to be one with Christ, to have the mind of Christ, they will become one with each other.

Denis O'Callaghan

Bridge over troubled waters

Readings: Ps 117:24-29. Rom 15:1-6; 12:9-13

This is the day that the Lord has made.
Let us rejoice. Alleluia. (Easter Liturgy)

A wedding is a great act of faith, a moment when a man and a woman make an act of trust in each other. It is nothing more or less than putting their lives and future in each other's hands. It must assuredly be the most amazing moment in their lives. It would be unrealistic to say that it does not contain an element of risk, but so does everything else we do, whether it be launching a boat or flying a kite or even driving a car. However, it would be a pity to spend too much time thinking of the risks, because marriage is a worthwhile adventure, a holy enterprise, a God-made arrangement.

Marriage is the giving of one person to another, a giving in which all is shared, all is enjoyed together. But for a successful marriage another element must be present, *caring*. Soon this magic of sharing and caring for each other will overflow into the sharing and caring for others. Marriage is not a selfish, two-centred institution, but an expanding, all-embracing love affair.

At birth we are set upon a bridge, and our days are spent crossing over this bridge to the other side, until the day we set foot into the next world. It is an immense bridge, very crowded with people, who are hustling and bustling each other along the way. And down below, under the bridge, there is a roaring torrent of water. We are all of us destined to spend our lives getting across this *bridge over troubled waters*. For some it is a very lonely and frustrating journey; they get lost in the crowd. Others lose heart and are tempted to throw themselves off the bridge. Others give up the struggle, and try to retrace their steps. But they forget that on this bridge there is no going back, and the traffic must move along in the one direction: forward.

Marriage provides the necessary prop for our human fears and weaknesses, as we cross over this bridge. Hand in hand, arm-in-arm, two people can do better than one. 'It is not good for man to be alone' on that bridge. Crossing over the bridge of life, they will meet many people along the way. They must keep their heads high, and face the right direction. They must encourage those who are wavering and hold out a helping hand to those who falter. Above all they must keep smiling, and share the joy that is in their hearts. God awaits us

63

all on the other side, and he gives us all the helps we need to cross the bridge. The secret of happiness is to share what we have with others, and to care for others. If we share and if we care, we shall cross the *bridge over troubled waters* safely, and help to bring many others along with us to the other side.

Mark Tierney OSB

Intimacy and mystery

Reading: Col 3:12-17

In human life there is a rhythm running from birth to death with important points in between. Marriage day is one of these.

The wedding itself is a human experience and the religious ceremony of the sacrament brings out the inner meaning of the wedding, putting us in touch with a mystery that is familiar but elusive. From the moment that a couple exchange their consent they will be known to each other, to us, their families and friends and to the world at large, as husband and wife. Already blending as man and woman, they will merge as husband and wife, merging as a couple without being submerged as individuals.

People belong together and share this world, this human life in various ways. Each becomes a full person only in sharing life with others. Intuitively we know that giving and receiving is part of being human. Sharing is not losing. Married life is a special way for man and woman to relate with an intimacy all its own. For every couple it entails sharing the joy and pain, the success and failure of the human struggle. It means learning how to be human together.

In the world we are in, or rather the world we are making, people are out of touch, feeling isolated and on their own even though physically near, losing personal touch in an impersonal world, searching for intimacy without knowing how to attain it.

Intimacy happens as two hearts meet, sharing the inner worlds of longings, fears, anxieties, joys, the things one is ashamed of or shy about, the experiences that make the eyes brighten or the body tighten. In everyone's heart is a powerful longing for closeness. Some are aware of this. Others only know it as loneliness or absence of meaning in life. The inescapable need to relate is more fundamental than the drive for power, pleasure or success. That explains why material security or status do not of themselves satisfy.

In marriage, couples learn to touch ever more deeply in being intimate in body, heart and mind. Through this they touch the mystery of each other. In so doing they reach towards the mystery at the heart of all, which we call God.

Tony Baggot SJ

65

Ever ancient, ever new

Readings: Gen 2:18-24. Jn 17:20-26

What happens in the marriage ceremony is something which has been part of human experience from the beginning of time – a man and a woman finding happiness, fulfilment and companionship in marriage. And yet, each marriage is entirely unique. For each couple it is *their* marriage, with the sharing of *their* gifts, *their* hopes, *their* lives which makes their oneness special. That is why the cry, 'This at last is bone of my bone and flesh of my flesh' is just as vivid and fresh today as it was at the dawn of history.

That unique oneness does not just happen. Their love has to be real and active. For that, there are no simple blueprints. This marriage is unique, not a mere copy of other people's marriages. It faces the future not knowing what lies ahead: 'for better for worse, for richer for poorer, in sickness and in health'.

We celebrate this marriage before God to express our faith that, in the unknown future, their loyalty, understanding and healing of one another is supported by God's power and love: that they live in God and God in them. We come here too in order to tell them that we believe in them and support them by our prayer and by our friendship.

Because their marriage is unique, it can support us: it can contribute to the richness of our lives. Their love and oneness will give them a strength and a wealth which will overflow from their home, in neighbourliness, in their relationship to their families and friends, in social concern, in their work.

We celebrate this wedding in the church because we believe that they are undertaking a mission to each other, to their family, to society and to the Church. We hope that many will believe through them and through the love they share and that many will be helped and healed by their friendship.

Although this marriage is unique, it shares with all marriages the call to mirror God's everlasting love. It does so, however, in their particular lives which will show God's love in new ways to people who might not otherwise see it. As we turn to the central moments of this ceremony, we do so with thanksgiving for their love, with prayer that this love will grow throughout their lives and bring many blessings to them and to all of us, and with hope that, having loved one another as Jesus loves us, they may be with him and see forever the glory which was his before the foundation of the world.

+Donal Murray

Secular reality – divine mystery

Readings: Hos 3:1-5. Ezek 16, 23. Eph 5:21-33

Marriage existed before the advent of Abraham and Jesus. It has been an enduring secular reality which, in the Judaeo-Christian tradition, has been taken up in the divine order. From the time of Hosea it was seen in the Old Testament as a symbol portraying the covenant of God. In the New Testament it was seen by Paul as a symbol of the relationship between Christ and the Church. So right up to our own day it is the secular reality that becomes a divine mystery.

If this is the case we have to ask continuously what is the secular reality of marriage today? It is in the depths of that reality that we shall find God's presence.

Marriage is changing in Western society, subtly, imperceptibly, but in a very marked way, and it is necessary to recognise in what way it is changing. The marriage that most of us were brought up with was characterised by clear and specific roles of spouses. The man went out to work, was the provider, the head of the family, and the source of authority. The woman was the bearer of children, subordinate to the man, looked after the house and the children. Provided the couple remained faithful to each other and raised their children in a permanent relationship, this was considered a good marriage. Today the pattern is altering. The massive emancipation of women has meant that the woman-man relationship has changed. The couple now attempt to relate to one another on a basis of equality, intimacy, with an emphasis on feelings and sexuality. As a result marriage becomes the second intimate relationship in life. The first was between ourselves and our parents when we learned the meaning of love, and the second is between ourselves and our spouse when we relive love in the relationship of marriage.

We know that the current marriage pattern of companionship has a very high degree of marital breakdown, but do we know what are its positive characteristics? What is the image of God that can be reflected in contemporary marriage? In the depths of the intimacy of the relationship there are three basic experiences, in which the image of God is situated, that are vital for the survival of the marriage.

The first experience is *sustaining*. The couple need to sustain each other materially as before, but in the intimacy of contemporary companionship marriage there has also to be emotional sustaining. The couple need to know each other in depth as they felt known and understood by their parents, and so communication is vital.

In the depths of this communication they reveal to each other their emotional wounds. These wounds come from their genetic make up and their upbringing. Genetically they may be more anxious, more depressed, more aggressive. As far as upbringing is concerned the most perfect parents leave a trail of hurt in terms of insecurity, the sense of rejection, feeling unloved, insecure, lacking confidence and self-esteem. Here the couple can help to *heal* each other. They give to each other a second opportunity to be loved and to have their wounds removed. There is more healing in marriage than in any other institution in society.

Finally, couples who nowadays remain married for 40/50 years change during that period. Unlike the traditional marriage, the contemporary marriage is not static. The couple can help each other to *grow*. There is no physical growth, but there is intellectual growth in which couples transform each other's intelligence with wisdom, and there is emotional growth into a greater capacity to love.

Thus the character of the secular reality of companionship marriage is intimacy, and in this intimacy sustaining, healing and growth are the channels of divine action.

Jack Dominian

For sustaining, healing and growth see Dominian J., *Marriage, Faith and Love,* Fontana.

5

Home-making

Open to life

Readings: Prov 24:3-4. Mt 25:31-46

Life offers no more awesome change than the transition from singlehood to parenthood. None of life's other experiences is so marvellously profound, so totally transforming. From girlhood to motherhood, from boyhood to fatherhood is an implosion into a new orbit. Parents become pro-Creators. God the Father graciously elicits their cooperation in a new creation. Their love is no longer turned inward on themselves but outward and open to life. And God said: 'Let us make man in our own image and likeness'. The fruit of their love is the image of all three, of father, of mother and God.

'Therefore, a man leaves his father and mother and cleaves to his wife and they become one flesh.' They mortgage themselves and their lives on a new home. Home is the warm love that breeds new life, cradles it through its vulnerable years and nurtures it for the outside world's harsher climate. Together, father and mother build a home, warm and comforting, strong and secure.

> By wisdom a house is built,
> and by understanding it is established;
> by knowledge the rooms are filled
> with all precious and pleasant riches (Prov 4:3-4)

The 'precious riches' make demands, demands only love could bear. Painful moments, fretful hours, anxious days, sleepless nights. Knowledge is being there to hold a sick child's hand. Understanding is wiping away the tears and being rewarded with a smile. Wisdom is double-edged. Children learn to grow up and parents rediscover their childhood. Home is the centre of the world and the promise of a better world to come.

Homelessness defines the needy, the lonely, the abandoned and the marginalised. Only home can fill their need. The nuclear family blossoms into the extended family, to share its warmth with the less fortunate. The word *home* is an acronym with a moral. H stands for for happiness. O stands for others. ME signifies self. The secret of a happy home is always to put others before self. Husband puts his wife first, and she her husband. Both put their children first and they their parents. All put neighbours first, especially those most in need.

Small wonder Christ chose the virtues of home for entry into the heavenly home:

'I was hungry and you gave me food, I was thirsty and you gave me drink, I was a stranger and you welcomed me, I was naked and you clothed me, I was sick and you visited me, I was in prison and you came to me' (Mt 25:35-36).

Children always assume their parents go to heaven. They should know with their privileged information. To parents, their children were 'the least of the brethren'.

Liam Swords

Where we all belong

Readings: 2 Kings 4:8-17. Prov 31:10-31. Jn 19:25-27

We all want to be the woman/man for others. Deep down in our hearts is the longing to be a parent, a spouse, a bread-winner, a minister of comfort, an instrument of hope.

Home enlarges us, extends us, brings out the best in us. It provides the setting in which we thrive and come fully alive. Or at least such is our ambition. Marriage is going public, giving oneself to another, identifying with spouse, relatives, friends.

Our age is hungry for the stability, security, peace and warmth of home. It takes two to make a home. Both must develop their capacities for self-giving, become ever more open to others, meet constant demands upon time and attention.

A satisfying experience of home life, to love and to be loved, to feel wanted by and to belong to others, is crucial for personal development.

Homemakers have the spirit of Ruth: 'Wherever you go I will go, wherever you live, I will live. Your people shall be my people, and your God, my God' (Ruth 1:16). Ruth, an honoured figure in the family tree of Jesus, is the mother *par excellence*. In her generosity she pushed open the door into a partnership with God that benefits us all.

The strength of married love is that it keeps open house for others, is untiringly hospitable, welcoming, ready to share with the stranger. Jewish families set a place at the passover table in the hope that the prophet Elijah would knock at the door and claim his seat around the festive board. The lighted Christmas candle in the window and the unlocked Irish door belong to a period untroubled by housebreaking and vandalism. To create a home of welcomes these days is a real challenge.

Fathers are breadwinners. Mothers dispense the fruits of labour. Bread graces the table, the bread of family and fellowship. Farmhouse meals were home-produced meals, celebrations of God's bounty and of our parents' labours. The tastes and smells of home retain part and parcel of each one of us. Parents channel their energies and ingenuity into homemaking. Children enjoy a cheerful love that knows no bounds. They absorb with fresh air and wholesome food the sound values of a living Christian tradition. To adapt a phrase of Saint-Exupéry, there is no savour like that of home-baked bread shared among your own people at the family table.

P J Brophy

Intimacy

Reading: Col 3:12-21

Intimacy is what sums up best of all the relationship between man and woman in marriage which is so tenderly described in Paul's words in Colossians. Marriage in our day has everything going for it. There is a move towards equality of the sexes, towards a change of responsibility and consequently towards greater intimacy. We used to learn about the three Rs – reading, 'riting, 'rithmetic. We overlooked the fourth and most important R which is relationship. The quality of family life is best judged by the quality of relationship between husband and wife, between parents and children; by the intimacy that obtains in the home; by the ability to 'be clothed with sincere compassion, in kindness and humility, gentleness and patience' (Col 3:12).

There are three words which describe this intimacy in marriage. The first is *sustaining*. It is a question more of emotional sustaining than of economic sustaining. Sensitivity is called for, which is being aware of what is going on inside the other person. We have to get to the feelings of the other, to their need for security, for understanding especially in times of acute distress. One of the most important things in life is the education of the feelings, the training of the heart.

The second word that describes this intimacy is *healing*. Husband and wife have an infinite capacity for healing each other and their children. The wounds and bruises in our personalities, whether they are caused by temperament or by upbringing, can be healed by a sensitive partner or parent. Prior to healing is the ability to listen and to hear the signals for help, affirmation and encouragement.

The third word that describes intimacy is *growth*. The couple can help each other to grow, not so much intellectually as in wisdom, love and creativity. One of the criticisms levelled against marriage today is that it is impossible to expect two individuals to live under the same roof for half a century without getting bored with each other. We have learned however that there is no limit to the possibility for growth in love. We can go on learning to grow in love until the last day of our lives.

Eltin Griffin OCarm

For sustaining, healing and growth, see Dominian J., *Marriage, Faith and Love*, Fontana.

The Trampoline

Readings: Jn 1:5. Lk 19:1-10, 11:33-36

> *A light that shines in the dark;*
> *a light that darkness*
> *could not overpower. (John 1:5)*

The coming together of two people, and their union in marriage, is a *light*, a sign of hope and encouragement, in a world which is much too full of darkness. This is a wonderful world, a beautiful world, and it is on such an occasion as this that we are assured of the triumph of truth and love and goodness over the forces of darkness. A wedding is a time when all the sham and drudgery and broken dreams of other times are shattered. It is a time to rejoice in the mystery of life, the mystery of love and the mystery of our human existence. It is above all a time to love, a time to live, and a time to think.

A family is more than a house or a home, it is more than a husband and wife, more than a mother and father. A family is nothing more than life going on. The marvellous thing about a family – the family circle – is that it can absorb the shocks of our worst moments. We need the family at all times of our lives: when we are teenagers, as a refuge and safe haven from the crazy, mixed-up, moody, rebellious, difficult world we live in; and when we are adults, we need the family as a solid base for all our enterprises. It is above all in the family that we feel accepted, where we are at our best and also at our worst. The family, like a trampoline, can absorb all our nastiness and all our foibles, and literally put us on our feet again, upright and steady. This newly formed family will provide a safe haven, a safe harbour, a beacon to light up the darkness and bring joy not just to themselves, but to many others as well.

The centre of any home is the family hearth, but much of the vitality and happiness will come from the hearts of those who live there. A number of years ago an old man was dying. He had never married, never travelled, never done very much. He said quite simply: 'Life passed me by'. What he meant was that he felt he had wasted his life, achieved nothing. But life never passes anyone by. It turned out that the old man had done a great amount during his life, for he had a soft heart, an open heart, a generous heart. And because of that he had unwittingly, almost unknowingly helped a considerable number of people. We should pray everyday for a soft heart, open to people. The heart is a landscape which is subject to darkness and light. We have to paint a bright and happy scene upon it, for our family circle will be the reflection of all that is within us.

Building a house is a simple matter, provided you have the money, the bricks and the mortar. Building a home is more difficult. It requires atmosphere, character and a great deal of endeavour. A house will reflect the genius of the architect and the builder; a home will reflect the personality of those who live there. May your house be built on a rock, solid and firm; may your home be built on love, generosity and an open heart. And may you both be happy in each other's company all the days of your lives.

Mark Tierney OSB

Friend go up higher

Readings: Song of Songs 5:8-16. Ps 45:10-17. Lk 14:7-11

Jesus was a great man for a wedding or a party of any kind. According to St John he worked his first miracle at a wedding in Cana, and he worked that first miracle so that the wedding guests could enjoy themselves. He was so happy at parties that even the disciples of John the Baptist asked why his disciples did not fast. Jesus replied that guests never fast as long as the bridegroom is with them.

A man who would compare himself to a bridegroom is a man who is fond of a wedding. He even went so far as to compare the kingdom of heaven, which was what he came to speak about, to a wedding feast. The wedding feast is a very pleasant picture of the heaven he invites us to; much more pleasant than the cartoon heaven in which old gentlemen in white dressing gowns play their individual harps on their individual clouds.

Even when he spoke of simple things like avoiding public disgrace, Jesus referred to a wedding feast. He warned his hearers not to head straight for the top table at a wedding in case some more important guest should turn up and leave them disgraced in front of those they had tried to impress.

Since Jesus was so happy at weddings, so at home among people in love, he is delighted to accept an invitation to come along to the feast.

He won't push himself, of course. He and his disciples turned up at Cana because they were invited, but if he is given an invitation he will certainly accept it. He would love to be invited to every day of this marriage for the rest of this couple's lives, but he still won't push himself forward. . . unless he is invited. Jesus Christ knows his place. It's in your hearts or nowhere at all.

Cathal & Norah O Boyle

Bread of life

Reading: Jn 6:30-40

During the years of the Second World War improvisation was essential for survival. Mother gathered together scraps of soap and melted them down in order that fresh bars of soap could be home-manufactured.

Then there was the smell of fresh bread wafting up through the house and the tiny egg-cup full of sugar, the day's ration.

Turf or peat had to be cut, dried and carted from the bog high on the 'Featherbed Mountain' overlooking Dublin city. There was no coal.

Father dug, for what seemed like hours, to plant potatoes and vegetables for the family table. Each morning we lined up dutifully to receive our daily dose of cod liver oil from him.

I recall with embarrassment the time I was tied to a tree by youthful companions during a game of 'cowboys and Indians' and having released myself, after what seemed like hours, running crying to be comforted by my mother.

Those words of Jesus, 'I am the bread of Life', speak of something more than the promised Eucharist.

Being the 'Bread of Life' for one another is the essence of home-making. It is sustaining presence, improvisation to meet each other's need, it is being comforted in distress.

To be the 'Bread of Life' for one another is to confidently expect mutual support and comfort. As Jesus promised to be the bread of life for us, we in turn have to be the bread of life for each other, particularly in marriage.

Martin Tierney

Christian marriage

Readings: Eph 5:21-33. 1 Jn 4:8. Lk 24:13-32. Mt 18:21-22

Many people ask what is distinctive about Christian marriage? If it is a secular reality marked by an inner world of sustaining, healing and growth, then are these experiences not open to everyone? What is distinctive about the word Christian?

In the Catholic tradition marriage is a sacrament, and in all the Christian churches it is something holy. The difference between the secular reality and the divine mystery is that for the Christian the ordinary becomes extraordinary. For the Christian couple the moment to moment experience of each other is a second to second experience of Christ. As the couple get up, wash, dress, have breakfast, go to work, take the children to school, look after the house, return for the evening meal, watch TV, go to bed and make love, all these human activities become encounters with Christ. But what does an encounter with Christ mean? The men who encountered Christ on the road to Emmaus had their eyes opened when they recognised him. Their whole vision of life changed. So it is with the couple who recognise Christ in each other.

This recognition brings the divine life into their life. It gives them the *motivation* to go on living when there are difficulties in the way. It encourages them to *forgive* repeatedly so that the relationship can be reopened and restored. It gives them *hope,* when things are going badly, to persevere. It helps them to cope with death as their basic belief in a life hereafter strengthens their conviction that they have not lost each other for good. The encounter with Christ in fact reshapes the quality of life.

But the Christian marriage is a symbol of more than the union between God and man, Christ and the Church. At the heart of the family is an encounter of persons. Husband encounters wife, parents encounter children, children encounter each other, and the family encounters the community. All these are encounters of love. Now the encounter of people in love is the essence of the Trinity. The Father encounters the Son, the Son encounters the Father, and the fount of their love for one another is the Spirit who encounters both in return. So the family is the little church whose members are in fact experiencing the trinitarian model of love. Whenever people meet each other in love there is a trinity in which love is the third person. Marriage does this superbly and it gives us a shadowy awareness of the Trinity in a unique way.

77

So Christian marriage is truly a secular reality in which God reigns. This God is invisible and not open to physical touch, but visible in the way that he influences the quality of relationship which truly reflects the image of God in man.

Jack Dominian

6

Interchurch Marriages

Perfectly in tune

Reading: Col 3:12-17

There is something deeply satisfying about harmony. A boy and a girl have come together from different Christian backgrounds to pledge loyalty, unity and love to each other for life. The harmony of the love and the presence of friends is a melodious chord in these days of discord and division.

One of the sadder aspects of life today is the spectacle of a people divided on how they perceive God. God sees all as brothers and sisters and it is that mutual love and respect that makes them recognised as the disciples of God in this age. For all that, there is too much mistrust, too much suspicion that there is some unsaintly intrigue in the process of a major takeover bid for the name of Christianity. Jesus Christ wanted community, not conformity. He wanted all to take him at his word, to step out in the path and Way he said he was, to be a reflection of the light of the world in the twilight of an earth darkened by the menacing clouds of war and endless sectarian divisions.

Today, two people found harmony in each other's love. Their marriage asks that Christ, who proved his love beyond all doubt, will be with them in the days and years that lie ahead. There is a deep Christian tradition behind both churches – a history of praise and witness to Christ, in different forms and dimensions, but the worship was of the one God and father of us all. Not only that, but this couple's love for each other has brought together a group of separated Christians who have all been enriched by friendships fostered in their common affection for both. This ceremony is rich indeed because, at this celebration of love, division and dissension have no place.

May your life together flourish and prosper. May you try always to be as good as God to each other and, in the wake of your love for each other, may the divisions among us, Christians of this land, disappear forever.

John J McCullagh

God's broken home

Reading: Jn 17:2-3, 20-26

Life is brittle. People break easily and in a myriad different ways. Broken limbs, broken hearts, broken lives, broken homes. Life is strewn with human wreckage. People, their lives and their loves, are hostages to fortune and fortune can often be capricious. The rain falls and the sun shines, as Christ so poignantly put it, equally on the just and the unjust. Like war-veterans, all carry scars. And scars take time to heal. If it is a family wound, it may take generations. When the human family breaks, it takes centuries to mend. As Humpty-Dumpty discovered, it may defy the best efforts 'of all the King's horses and all the King's men' to put it together again.

History suggests that few scars are so deep and so difficult to cure as those left by religious wounds. Today's headlines give brutal confirmation of that. Jew against Arab, Shi'ite Muslim against Christian Phalangist, Catholic against Protestant. The Middle East, the cradle of the three great religious families, Christian, Jew and Muslim, is now the world's cockpit. God's own broken family.

A broken family is a failure of love that only love can mend. When two children of God's broken home seal their love in marriage, God's healing hand delicately resets the broken pieces. Their love for each other overcomes the festering prejudices of the ages and releases God's gentle healing. They are frontier people, building their home astride a border of beliefs. The border that divides men's minds can only be crossed by love.

Theirs is an ecumenical miracle. Their family is the domestic church, a church where two traditions give birth to children, free at last from the centuries-old scars of religious dissension. In their home, if Christ is Lord, God's broken home is marvellously restored. Christ's parting prayer, 'that they may be one', finds here a perfect answer.

Liam Swords

Lighthouses of hope

Reading: Ex 1:16-22

Easter Thursday's prayer runs: 'Father, you gather the nations to praise your name. May all who are reborn in baptism be one in faith and love.'

An interchurch marriage presupposes a conversion experience which focusses upon what it means to be christened and now united in love with another christened person of a different tradition. How to be true to oneself, and to one's tradition, and to Jesus our common Lord, challenges both partners and their home faith communities.

The starting point in any discussion on marriage must be how to do justice to the legitimate expectations of the spouses. We reject stereotypes of feminine roles imposed by separate education and cultural associations. It was all too facile to assume yesterday that the grace of the sacrament would smooth out difficulties that should have been resolved by frank discussion and agreed solutions. Obedience was a cover-up for domination.

Where the common ground of a shared faith and a clearly defined tradition is not present, couples must have, or seek to acquire, a deeper knowledge of themselves, an awareness of what divides them, and a solid conviction about the central core Christian doctrines upon which their churches agree.

An interchurch marriage starts off under the shadow of potential discord and disruption. The very faith in Jesus Christ which should unite them could divide them. Silence about religious differences between them would be an evasion, not a solution. Much of what separates Christians is due to non-religious factors and apologetic attitudes. The aftermath of religious controversy lingers on in how truths are presented. Healing is our need. Contaminated wells must be sealed.

When faith in Jesus Christ is understood to be a personal encounter, a meeting of hearts more easily follows. A deepening appreciation of the other's position must be the constant aim.

Interchurch marriage can be a grace, enabling the partners to look closely at their own position and distinguish between the truths by which they live and the merely local colour of denominational expressions. The spouses seeing one another in a relationship with Jesus attach themselves more closely to him and to one another. Jesus becomes the bond of union, never the source of dissension in their married life. It is the Lord in whom they place their trust. They are

81

workers for the unity God wills.

Those who look to God together in interchurch marriages witness to the yet-to-be-achieved unity that is God's will for his church. Their calling is to be unity workers, *foyers de l'unité*. *I* must give place to *we* and all to discovering what God wills.

The way ahead may be unclear. The path to be followed is one of faith, service and acceptance of the restraints imposed by divisions. Households dedicated to unity are lighthouses of hope in what may otherwise be a bleak scene. Couples in an interchurch marriage, through their genuine concern for unity, respond to the prayer of Jesus on the night before he died that all his followers 'be so completely one that the world will realise that it was you who sent me' (Jn 17:23). They authenticate the presence of Jesus in their marriage.

P J Brophy

Welcome friend

Readings: Mk 9:33-41. Jn 17:1-26

François Mauriac made one of his characters say that in a certain part of France it was not so much a matter of two people as of two forests marrying each other. Family honour, the dowry, the succession of property, could become so important.

For most of us property or money is not that kind of problem; we are not tempted to believe that on a sunny June morning it is really two farms or two business enterprises that are marrying each other. Sometimes, though, we may be caught up with the idea that two churches are marrying each other.

What we are celebrating is the joyful union of two persons who have shown that they are capable of reaching out in love beyond the bounds which other people have set for them. We may say, 'You must find your love here, or here'; but love does not recognise boundaries like that. Love will find its own, no matter what barriers of class, money, nationality or institution we put up against it.

Should we not be happy because of that?

When our Lord was on earth reaching out to his friends he joyfully went beyond all the barriers which people had set up. Some of them were set up by very wise people who confidently believed that by setting up barriers they were protecting their own people, or their faith, even protecting God, and to some extent they succeeded.But there comes a time when barriers have to be breached not by aggression but by love.

So Jesus was joyfully demonstrative of his friendships. The Roman soldier, the Samaritan woman, Mary Magdalen, a tax collector. In each case he pulled aside a formidable barrier, a barrier set up for the most honourable reasons, and reached the human person whom he loved. Caution is good, but in the end love makes caution unnecessary.

In our marriage two friends welcome each other into hearts and lives. Two families welcome each other as friends and allies. We penetrate each other's defences; nothing about us now can be completely private, completely our own. We share, or our life withers. Christian communities are like this. They are nothing if they are not welcoming. It is the Christian's whole life to give welcome. One Christian community opens its mind and heart to another.

Thank God for it.

Our worship is a sign of all this. The presence at our marriage of those who lead, inspire and minister to our Christian worship according to our different traditions is a sign of our welcome and our acceptance of welcome.

Joyful welcome. Joyful acceptance.

We Christians in face of such a miracle of reunion do not say, 'Welcome Stranger.' We say, 'Welcome Friend.'

Desmond Wilson

7

Mature marriages

Forget the cornflakes!

Readings: Eph 2:4-10. Ps 100. Mt 5:13-16

Two scientists spent six months together in a small tent studying weather patterns at the North Pole. On returning home they were interviewed on radio about the difficulties of their trip. The interviewer asked one of them if differences in ideology or scientific approach had caused problems. 'No,' the man replied, 'what really drove me crazy was the way he ate his cornflakes!'

Like it or not, we are creatures of habit. As time passes we develop our individual ways of doing and saying things, and we become quite content with, indeed oblivous to our personal collection of quirks and idiosyncrasies. We can be most understanding, tolerant, even amused by the habits of others, as long as we don't have to live with them.

But when two people of whatever age discover that their love for each other calls them to marriage, the accidentals of their lives must yield to the demands of their love. There is an inescapable tension there – on the one hand the longer you live without having to share your life with another the more difficult it is to yield the accidentals, yet your greater wisdom would have taught that the same accidentals are not the essence of a marriage. Your experience would also have told you that marriage is not so much about *finding* the right person,but *being* the right person.

You have had more time than most to prepare yourselves for this day and for your shared life in the future. You have enjoyed different experiences, met many different people, visited different places, worked in different situations. But now as you pledge your love to each other for the remainder of your lives, let those differences take on a positive value. Enrich and complete yourselves as you learn from each other's experience. Thank God for each other's past, the joys and the pains, because they have fashioned the person with whom you fell in love.

Dermod McCarthy

The deliberate lover

Readings: Prov 31:8-31. 1 Cor 13. 2 Pet 1:2-21

When St Paul described love in the marvellous thirteenth chapter of his first Letter to the Corinthians what he was writing about was something noble, something infinitely attractive, and something – dare we say it? – of which only people with many years' experience of loving could achieve.

Sudden flights of fancy, that is not what St Paul meant. Sudden attraction which leaves a lover sighing every day more and more until the consummation of love and then sighing less and less every day thereafter, that is not what he was talking about either.

He was talking about the love of people who have endured enough to make them feel the need and the blessedness of forgiveness; the love of people who have accumulated enough gifts, material and spiritual, to make what they give well worth receiving. Who have learned from many a loving experience, and many a bruising one, what it means to love and respect our friends not because they are young, not because they are old, but because at this moment they are exactly as they are, God's creation, God's redemption, filled with the Holy Spirit.

The person who loves with the love that Paul speaks about is the one who gives not on impulse but with the quiet deliberation of a lover who has come to know the full value of the gift.

Christ's people will find joy in life, in youth, in maturity, in old age, in each and every phase of life; will recognise that God's joy often comes directly to us from him but is most often mediated to us by others. Our constant prayer is that at every phase of our lives God may bless us with the companionship of someone whose love for us will be the channel through which at that time God's grace and beauty will touch us. We see each other's beauty , each other's goodness, we feel each other's warm affection, we treasure all these good gifts which God allows us to share. We are happy indeed if, at all phases of our life, he has given us such a person as a companion.

One of the great thoughts we have when celebrating the marriage union of two of our friends who have given their mature love to each other is that what we celebrate and give thanks for today is the hope we have for the future; a hope not blind but founded upon years of faith and love.

Desmond Wilson

8
Anniversaries

Pure gold

Reading: Tobit 14:13-16. Mt 7:21, 24-25

Early in the day it was whispered that we should set sail in a boat, only thou and I, and never a soul in the world would know of this our pilgrimage to no country and to no end. – Rabindrinath Tagore.

Fifty years of existence in a structure so time-prone as the union of human life and human love calls for a special sort of celebration, and for once time is not the enemy but the celebrant.

That this celebration should be called golden is mankind's tribute to its quality. No metal is mined deeper in human history and consciousness. It is and has been the object of desires and dreams, the reward of superlative achievement, the touchstone of worth, the measure of value in all our exchanges. After so long a time the hallmark may well have faded on the plain gold ring with which this man wed this woman fifty years ago, but today time itself has assayed the marriage which the ring made and marked it as genuine.

The guests on their wedding morning shared their joy. It was then the joy of a hopeful departure. We the guests on their golden wedding morning share their joy too but it is a different joy – the joy of an arrival and of hope fulfilled. The wishes made and the hopes expressed at wedding breakfasts seem sometimes in their exaggeration and vehemence to be tinged with fear, for we know that human happiness has a high mortality rate. So the wishes for the success of a marriage are pitched high and we tell each other what a lovely couple they are, as if with the strength of words to storm the citadels of the future. But the silent artillery of time is unfortunately not spiked by good wishes. And so part of the joy of this golden wedding is that for once our wishes have come true. It is not just one couple's triumph – it is a triumph for all of us and we have so few.

In photographs of golden wedding groups the old couple seem often to be slightly, tolerantly, amused by the fuss. We seem almost to exhibit them as trophies and they let us. They enjoy and are happy in their children's celebration of the event, but there is a secret quality to their happiness that not even their children know. Children nearly always think of their parents as existing only from the time that they have known them, but this man and this woman share times and secrets and memories that are theirs and only theirs. In Yeat's words they:

> . . . have found the best that life can give,
> Companionship in those mysterious things
> That make a man's soul or a woman's soul
> Itself and not some other soul.

Fifty and more years of reality and grace have been mediated to each through the other. The family has grown out of the basic unit of their marriage, but their marriage has not lost its identity in the greater family unit. It has preserved its own individual and secret being unshared. So out of their meaning for each other, from the years that are locked away from all outsiders they smile to each other and share their happiness with all.

Thomas Waldron

Reprinted from *The Furrow*.

sunshine, joy or promise. The ageless Christ is here today and is proud that his grace and presence has worked in this miracle of love. That miracle has made this battle-bruised world a brighter place down through the years in the lived-out promise of that distant altar together.

John J McCullagh

Two good forgivers

Readings: Tobit 8:4-8. Ps 103. Col 3:12-17. Jn 17:20-23

From the mountains, on a clear day, the whole city spreads like a vast carpet beneath. In the middle distance rise the spires and monuments which have been landmarks for centuries, but around the perimeter, new housing estates stretch like concrete tentacles into the surrounding countryside. The houses are lookalike little boxes, on identical roads, drives, avenues and crescents.

Identical, that is, from the outside. But what about the lives of the people inside? What type of drama is being played out in each of those houses? Perhaps in some it is a suspense-filled thriller, in others a medieval morality play with one partner forever playing God. Maybe a neo-Shakespearean tragedy or a Feydeau comedy. Sadly in some it may be almost complete silence. In the majority, there is no acting but instead two people working hard at understanding one another, shaping their lives together, and being open and forgiving people.

Look back on the past and see into which category your marriage fits. Has it improved with age? Has your love for each other deepened since the day you wed? What role have you given to Christ in your marriage? One of the great similarities between Christianity and marriage is that, for Christians, they both get better as we get older. Is that your experience?

After his resurrection, Christ said, 'Whose sins you shall forgive they are forgiven'. This is more than simply an institutional text for the sacrament of reconciliation. It is first a call to be a forgiving people. Hence we say, 'I confess to Almighty God, *and to you my brothers and sisters,* that I have sinned. . .' Now if Christ calls his Church to be a forgiving community, it should be supremely true within a marriage and a family, which is the Church in microcosm. Someone once said,'Marriage is the union of two good forgivers'.

May this anniversary celebration help to chisel that slogan into your lives.

Dermod McCarthy

be lived. There will be again old difficulties and new hazards, but the road from Emmaus is lit with a new assurance.

In their walking together this husband and wife have, of course, known the dissillusionment and the disappointment which are part of all journeys to Emmaus. They have survived temptations, casual and sudden, of monotony and loneliness and curiosity, and the longing for adventure down a thousand by-ways. Some they have faced together and some individually but always with that other whom they met on the road. He has been with them together for a quarter of a century. These two have lived together and broken bread together for twenty-five years and they have known him in the breaking of bread.

Thomas Waldron

Reprinted from *The Furrow*.